302.23 Med

The media's influence on society /
$27.80   on1268332620

At Issue

The Media's Influence on Society

Other Books in the At Issue Series

COVID-19 and Other Pandemics
Food Security
Genocide
Is America a Democracy or an Oligarchy?
Money Laundering
Nuclear Anxiety
Open Borders
Pandemics and Outbreaks
Partisanship
Policing in America
The Politicization of the Supreme Court

At Issue

The Media's Influence on Society

Andrew Karpan, Book Editor

Published in 2022 by Greenhaven Publishing, LLC
353 3rd Avenue, Suite 255, New York, NY 10010

Copyright © 2022 by Greenhaven Publishing, LLC

First Edition

All rights reserved. No part of this book may be reproduced in any form without permission in writing from the publisher, except by a reviewer.

Articles in Greenhaven Publishing anthologies are often edited for length to meet page requirements. In addition, original titles of these works are changed to clearly present the main thesis and to explicitly indicate the author's opinion. Every effort is made to ensure that Greenhaven Publishing accurately reflects the original intent of the authors. Every effort has been made to trace the owners of the copyrighted material.

Cover image: Rawpixel.com/Shutterstock

Library of Congress Cataloging-in-Publication Data

Names: Karpan, Andrew, editor.
Title: The media's influence on society / Andrew Karpan [editor].
Description: First edition. | New York : Greenhaven Publishing, 2022. |
  Series: At issue | Includes bibliographical references and index. |
  Audience: Ages 15+ | Audience: Grades 10-12 | Summary: "This volume examines differing viewpoints on what can reasonably be expected of the media, the effects of the internet on the media, and the various impacts the media has on society—including political, cultural, and economic."— Provided by publisher.
Identifiers: LCCN 2020049080 | ISBN 9781534508231 (library binding) | ISBN
  9781534508224 (paperback) | ISBN 9781534508248 (ebook)
Subjects: LCSH: Journalism—Objectivity—United States—Juvenile
  literature. | Journalism—Social aspects—United States—Juvenile
  literature. | Mass media—Objectivity—United States—Juvenile
  literature.
Classification: LCC PN4888.O25 M453 2022 | DDC 302.23/0973—dc23
LC record available at https://lccn.loc.gov/2020049080

Manufactured in the United States of America

Website: http://greenhavenpublishing.com

Contents

Introduction   7

1. Corporate Interests Should Not Overshadow the Responsibility to Inform the Public   11
   Julie A. Demorest
2. Social Media Has Changed Journalism for the Better   19
   Andrea Carson
3. Snowden's Whistleblowing Prompted Public Awareness   24
   Ewen MacAskill and Alex Hern
4. The Public Wants Unbiased News   30
   Amy Mitchell, Katie Simmons, Katerina Eva Matsa, and Laura Silver
5. The Media Feedback Loop   35
   Jonathan Stray
6. Media Reform Is Essential to Democracy   43
   Robert W. McChesney
7. Investigative Journalism Can Save Lives   55
   Scott Simon
8. The Media's Role in Promoting Tech Companies   58
   Pew Research Center
9. Celebrities Have the Power to Push for Privacy from the Media   62
   Marcel Berlins
10. Analyzing How Media Covers a Debate   67
    The Roosevelt Institute
11. A Global Fast Food Workers' Movement Is Bolstered by Media   78
    Annelise Orleck
12. Politicians Use "Fake News" to Discredit Media   85
    Andrea Carson and Kate Farhall

13. Americans Are Divided in Their Trust of the News
    Media 90
    Jeffrey Gottfried, Galen Stocking, Elizabeth Grieco,
    Mason Walker, Maya Khuzam, and Amy Mitchell
14. We Live in a Post-Truth Era 93
    Ahmed Al Sheikh
15. The Internet Changes Reporting, Too 99
    Aleks Krotoski
16. Fake News Shakes Americans' Confidence 103
    Michael Dimock
17. The Center Loses Hold 107
    Michael Griffin

Organizations to Contact 115
Bibliography 121
Index 126

Introduction

Fake news, everyone! Few phrases better capture the precarious status of media today. The cry of "fake news" blurs what is true and what is not, encouraging mistrust of the Fourth Estate and laying the groundwork for political misdeeds.

The words themselves were plucked from the end of a 2016 BuzzFeed headline: "How Teens in the Balkans Are Duping Trump Supporters with Fake News."[1] The story detailed the actions of hackers in North Macedonia, who had been making a small living penning news articles with headlines like "Pope Francis Forbids Catholics from Voting for Hillary" and "Robert De Niro Switches to Trump." The stories mattered, and yet they didn't matter. They were shared hundreds, thousands of times before disappearing. They were to be dismissed, we were told, and they repeatedly were until all that remained of them was their stern two-word dismissal, whose echo was handily reappropriated against entirely unrelated reports that were unflattering, potentially damaging, and cast a harsh light on their subjects.

This revealed the ways in which media influences society and, in some ways, how the relationship has become a bidirectional one. Stories about the lives we live are told by journalists and by bloggers, by movies, and by pop songs. They get turned into phrases and memes, repeated without context until they become standalone cultural artifacts, words in the dictionary whose origins are of interest only to specialists. Think of it as the ambient noise of the culture, the way words and fortunes get made, a back and forth game of telephone that details the whole of human history.

But, we're also told, people are trusting the media less these days. In 2016, the same year BuzzFeed reported on the literal fictions being spun abroad for readers at home, a Gallup poll found that only 32 percent of people who responded in the United

States said they feel confident that media outlets are reporting "the news fully, accurately and fairly," a record low for the polling organization.[2] (By 2019, that percent would slug back upward to 41 percent.[3])

The number of people reporting those stories seems to have plummeted, too. Another study, courtesy of a Pew Research Center analysis of Bureau of Labor Statistics data, says that overall employment in newsrooms dropped 23 percent between 2008 and 2019.[4] The numbers, of course, measure only mainstream outlets: the newspapers tasked with keeping city hall accountable and the broadcast news stations that report their findings on television. Increasingly, it seemed, people were turning to media made elsewhere: on YouTube channels headquartered in bedrooms and social media posts whose origins were hard to trace.

It's no small coincidence, perhaps, that this same period of time gave rise to a massive cultlike conspiracy theory called QAnon, spread initially on the decidedly non-mainstream social media website 4chan. Proposing an entirely alternative network of news stories, the movement offered readers something that bore little relationship to stories covered elsewhere. That these were largely considered conspiracy theories of dubious provenance mattered little to its believers, and its spread in the late 2010s seemed symptomatic of that wider distrust in media, that larger sense that reporters were getting something wrong and were involved in a collective cabal to hide something from ordinary people. "The rise in conspiratorial thinking is the product of several interrelated trends: declining trust in institutions; demise of local news; a social-media environment that makes rumor easy to spread and difficult to debunk," wrote Charlotte Alter in *Time*.[5]

The medium of all these new messages was the internet. It was the internet that brought down newsrooms who now had to compete for clicks with social media networks like Facebook and Twitter. It was the internet that published the "fake news" and the "alternative facts." It was the internet that turned media from a set number of publications, publishers, and TV networks into an infinite number of websites and content farms of sometimes dubious origin. But it was also through email that a whistleblower named Edward Snowden began communicating the details of a massive surveillance program the United States was conducting in coordination with intelligence agencies around the world. Political movements of all kinds, from revolutions against totalitarian governments to collective efforts to increase the minimum wage, went online to find their fellow travelers.

And it's just as much of a mistake to assume that the fake news is coming maliciously from afar. "The largest obstacle to reliable news and information," former MSNBC producer Ariana Pekary writes in the *Columbia Journalism Review*, is that "hardly any programming decision is made without considering how it will 'rate.'"[6] The reporters who are left cover the stories that will be read by the most people. Stories about the gilded lives of celebrities, the protests that turn violent, and the extremes at the far ends of the political spectrum are produced to evoke fear in the minds of most watchers. As a whole, the stories we are watching have started to feel darker, an effect compounded by the small glowing screens we are watching them on.

The turn to extremes has made media more polarized. The widely held feelings of distrust toward the media have become particularized to the politics of the viewer. Another Pew study, conducted in early 2020, found that no mainstream news source is trusted by more than half of all American adults.[7] People who identify as Democrat trust MSNBC and CNN, and people who identify as Republican trust only Fox News, the researchers say. In lieu of a shared understanding of news events and their relative importance, there are echo chambers that pick and choose what their viewers would find most agreeable. When President Trump faced his first impeachment in the Senate, CNN and MSNBC aired the trial live while Fox News ran its "regular bloc of opinion programming."[8]

The authors of the diverse viewpoints contained in *At Issue: The Media's Influence on Society* are all trying to grapple with what those changes mean for societies around the world, whether it's the efforts of big businesses to change media coverage in the United States or the efforts of a ruling political party in India to silence critical coverage of an economic crash. They explore the ways that society gets short-shrifted by the media it consumes. For these writers, media is how they measure democracy, a thermostat on the information that voters are taking in before heading to the ballot box.

Endnotes

1. Craig Silverman and Lawrence Alexander, "How Teens in the Balkans Are Duping Trump Supporters with Fake News," BuzzFeed News, November 3, 2016. https://www.buzzfeednews.com/article/craigsilverman/how-macedonia-became-a-global-hub-for-pro-trump-misinfo
2. Art Swift, "Americans' Trust in Mass Media Sinks to New Low," Gallup, September 14, 2016. https://news.gallup.com/poll/195542/americans-trust-mass-media-sinks-new-low.aspx. The story is cited as helping popularize "fake news" in: Mike Wendling, "The (Almost) Complete History of 'Fake News,'" BBC, January 22, 2018. https://www.bbc.com/news/blogs-trending-42724320
3. Megan Brenan, "Americans' Trust in Mass Media Edges Down to 41%," Gallup, September 26, 2019. https://news.gallup.com/poll/267047/americans-trust-mass-media-edges-down.aspx
4. Elizabeth Grieco, "U.S. Newspapers Have Shed Half of Their Newsroom Employees Since 2008," Pew Research Center, April 20, 2020. https://www.pewresearch.org/fact-tank/2020/04/20/u-s-newsroom-employment-has-dropped-by-a-quarter-since-2008
5. Charlotte Alter, "How Conspiracy Theories Are Shaping the 2020 Election—and Shaking the Foundation of American Democracy," *Time*, September 10, 2020. https://time.com/5887327/conspiracy-theories-2020-election/
6. Ariana Pekary, "CNN Public Editor: The Only Question in News Is 'Will It Rate?'" *Columbia Journalism Review*, September 2, 2020. https://www.cjr.org/public_editor/cnn-public-editor-the-only-question-in-news-is-will-it-rate.php
7. Mark Jurkowitz, Amy Mitchell, Elisa Shearer, and Mason Walker, "U.S. Media Polarization and the 2020 Election: A Nation Divided," Pew Research Center, January 24, 2020. https://www.journalism.org/2020/01/24/u-s-media-polarization-and-the-2020-election-a-nation-divided/
8. Oliver Darcy, "Instead of Airing the Impeachment Trial, Fox News Fed Viewers Pro-Trump Opinion in Prime Time," CNN, January 24, 2020. https://www.cnn.com/2020/01/23/media/fox-news-impeachment-coverage/index.html

1

Corporate Interests Should Not Overshadow the Responsibility to Inform the Public

Julie A. Demorest

The Institute for Applied and Professional Ethics is a research school at Ohio University that works on creating and articulating techniques for ethical behavior.

On some level, news is the prototypical public good. Because of that, it's also big business. The media sector of most Western countries is dominated by some of the largest companies in the world and is reliant on many of the rest for advertising revenue. But great power ought to beget greater responsibility, and such responsibility is sometimes betrayed. This author suggests a media stewardship that finds its voice in the ethical legacy of communitarianism and the pragmatism of John Dewey, an early twentieth-century voice of civic goodliness.

There is no denying that news media is big business. The complete coverage of stories and investigative reports are certainly at risk with the rise of media as a business, rather than strictly a service to the public. Over the past few years, there have been a number of cases where television stations or news publications have killed news stories or forced reporters to slant stories due to pressure from advertisers or those in power at the news. This paper will attempt to examine the relationship between

"Corporate Interests and Their Impact on News Coverage," by Julie A. Demorest, Ohio University, July 27, 2009. Reprinted by permission.

social responsibility and news editors, and apply ethical theories to explain what should and can be done. Should editors have the power to kill or slant stories, depending on their own interests or those of their advertisers?

Literature Review

A number of books and articles investigated the relationship between corporate and advertising interests and news coverage. In the May/June 2000 issue of *Columbia Journalism Review*, Lowell Bergman wrote an article entitled, "Network television news: With fear and favor." Bergman sums up his findings by saying, "Executives of the network news divisions say that they will report any story of public interest and import without fear or favor, without considering its potential commercial consequences. They say that, but they do not believe it" (p. 50).

Karl Idsvoog's journal article, "TV sitting on stories to improve ratings," claims that "the decision on when (or if) to run a piece is no longer determined just by asking is the report concise, clear, and well produced; is it fair, thorough, and accurate? There are now more critical questions. What's the lead-in? Where do we place the promotion? Will it deliver better numbers on Monday or Wednesday?" (Idsvoog, p. 38). However, he adds that "in the long run, adhering to a higher standard of ethics delivers a higher standard of performance" (p. 39).

Carol Guensburg examines the ethical dilemmas of news reporting that involve the media agency's owner in the December 1998 issue of *American Journalism Review* (p. 10). In "When the story is about the owner," she determines that it is up to the individual journalists and news operations to continue reporting important stories, regardless of the impact they may have on corporate or advertising interests (Guensburg, p. 11).

American Journalism Review's October 1998 article by Jane Kirtley, "Second-guessing news judgment," looks at the issue of FCC regulations of news coverage (p. 86). She notes that having the governmental agency get involved in news coverage would likely lead to the consequence that "broadcasters will be discouraged from covering controversial issues at all" (Kirtley, p. 86).

In addition to these and many other articles referencing corporate interests in the media, an organization called Project Censored does annual research to "explore and publicize stories of national importance on issues that have been overlooked or under-reported by the mainstream news media" (Jensen, p. 14).

Body

The relationship between social responsibility and news editors must have a very delicate balance. As stated, news is a business that depends on high ratings and advertising dollars for its survival. However, the news media is also a social organization responsible for informing and educating the public. Corporate interests are important, but the guiding principle for news organizations should be the responsibility to inform the public. News editors have the huge task of determining what stories are told on their news programs or in their publications. The interests of upper management, owners, and outside advertisers make the editors' decisions even more difficult.

In 1969, the Federal Communications Commission said that "rigging or slanting the news is a most heinous act against the public interest" (Kirtley, p. 86). Yet, it happens—all the time. Two particular cases are especially applicable. The first involves Lowell Bergman, former executive producer of CBS's *60 Minutes*. As executive producer, Bergman was intimately involved in the 1995 Brown & Williamson situation, when *60 Minutes* decided not to air a report on Jeffrey Wigand. Wigand, former vice president of Brown & Williamson, claimed that the company kept the truth about tobacco's harmful properties hidden from the public (Bergman, p. 50). He claimed that CBS self-censored itself to avoid a potential lawsuit from Brown & Williamson. Bergman also added that while working for ABC news he discovered that it was against "ABC code" to do an enterprise story about a major advertiser or supplier or to do a critical story on the owner of an NFL team (p. 51).

The second example directly showing how corporate interests impact news coverage took place in 1997. Jane Akre and Steve Wilson, award-winning investigative reporters for WTVT-13 in Tampa, Florida, were fired in December 1997 after they refused to broadcast false reports. Akre and Wilson had been working on a series of reports about a controversial growth hormone being injected into dairy cows for months, and the reports were scheduled to air beginning February 24, 1997. On the eve of the first broadcasts, the reports were pulled from the airwaves after Monsanto (maker of the hormone) complained to Fox Television, parent company of WTVT-13. WTVT management reviewed the reports, found no errors, and rescheduled their broadcasts. Monsanto lawyers sent a threatening letter to Fox's news division head, and the reports were postponed once again. In the nine months that followed, Akre and Wilson were ordered to rewrite the story with false information more than 80 times, none of which were acceptable to Fox executives. Akre and Wilson threatened to tell the FCC "of a false, distorted, or slanted news report that she reasonably believed would violate the prohibition against intentional falsification or distortion of the news on television." They were ultimately fired in December 1997 (Trigoboff, p. 27).

Instances such as these, where corporate interests override the public's need to know, most likely occur quite frequently. "Almost all media owners have friends who are given preferential treatment in news stories—friends whose ranks include advertisers, politicians, relatives, and acquaintances" (Armao, p. 46). Media critic Ben Bagdikian noted in an article that media organizations often pull back stories when they might offend advertisers (Winch, p. 132). He also stated that "no commercial power should dominate the news—just as no state power should" (Goldstein, p. 25).

In *Critical Studies in Mass Communication*, Matthew Ehrlich explained one of the factors accounting for trivial, superficial, and often inaccurate reporting—the "competitive ethos," which he defined as a "powerful, taken-for-granted set of norms within the community of television newsworkers" (p. 196). People who work in the news business have an unwritten set of codes, and they tend to base their work on them. One of those "codes" is that news is "whatever the competition is covering" (Krajicek, p. 184). This leads to a homogenization of the news, with all programs taking on a similar shape.

Another problem with news coverage is that media managers often appear to design news "based on what interests the public rather than what is in the best interests of the public" (Winch, p. 131). Sensationalism in news has certainly been a deterrent to credible and accurate reporting. The great news anchor Walter Cronkite has said that "the networks now do news as entertainment" (McCartney, p. 44). The public wants to see the wildest, craziest, and most outlandish news stories—not necessarily the stories that would have the greatest impact on their lives.

The "competitive ethos" factors listed above indicate one of the reasons why the role of the news editor is so crucial. It is up to the news editor and his team of editors to determine what is important to the public on a "need to know" and "right to know" basis, with "want to know" and "don't necessarily want to know, but need to show it to the public to gain ratings" much less important.

In his book, *The Media Monopoly*, Ben Bagdikian says that "because the country's top editors are being integrated into the management imperatives of the corporation, journalists, through their editors, become less responsible for the integrity of the news and more for the profitability of the whole enterprise. That is not journalism. It is advertising and marketing. Combining journalism with advertising and marketing ultimately will destroy the integrity of the news" (Edge, p. 197).

There is no clear-cut answer to the social responsibility and corporate interests conflict. Adopting a communitarian ethic based on the needs of society would probably make editors' decisions easier. Communitarianism insists that "mass-media structures make a decisive break with individualistic capitalism"

(Christians, p. 14). Deni Elliott's three nonnegotiable principles of journalism should apply to news editors and management as well, and are especially applicable to determining content of television news (Christians, p. 55). Her first principle is that "news reports should be accurate, balanced, relevant, and complete" (Christians, p. 55). Truth is the most important factor in news, so if a story is not honest, it should not be news. The second principle is that "journalists share the principle that reporting should avoid harm" (Christians, p. 55). While journalists should only report stories that avoid harm (and not cause it), they should also be careful to report stories that would possibly cause, or allow, harm to occur if not reported. Elliott's third principle for journalists is "to report information that viewers and readers need to know" (Christians, p. 56). As stated previously, it is essential that the news media provide vital information to the American public. The media has a social responsibility to share its wealth of information, especially when the news would have a direct impact on lives.

The pragmatic thought of John Dewey could be applied to this ethical dilemma as well. In his book, *Democracy and Education*, Dewey identifies four Theories of Morals: the inner and the outer, the opposition of duty and interest, intelligence and character, and the social and the moral (Dewey, 1916). The opposition of duty and interest is directly applicable to the corporate interests/news media dilemma. The opposition of duty and interest is defined as distinguishing the difference between acting on principle and acting on interest. Dewey explains acting on principle as acting "disinterestedly, according to a general law, which is above all personal considerations (1916). Acting on interest is "to act selfishly, with one's own personal profit in view" (Dewey, 1916). A news organization choosing to run a story that negatively impacts an important advertiser would be seen as acting on principle. The news organization would be acting without interest and above their personal considerations of how their jobs and profits might be impacted. Choosing not to run the story would be acting on interest, with personal and professional profits in clear view.

Summary

This paper attempted to explain that corporate interests are having a large impact on what the news media report to the American public, and theorized about how the situation could be changed. Adopting a communitarian ethic would allow the news media to more accurately and completely report the news that is important to the daily lives of Americans.

Conclusion

Corporate interests are important, but the guiding principle for news organizations should be the responsibility to inform the public. In *The Messenger's Motives*, John L. Hulteng stated that "the central, ruling ethic of journalism is to report the news of the world dependably and honestly" (p. 171). Given that corporate interests do play a role in what appears on television news and in newspapers, what should be done? The news giants and advertisers aren't going to go away, so the public and news media need to share the social responsibility. The American public needs to realize that the news media aren't always giving the complete story. They should not rely solely on television and print news media for information, but should look elsewhere for alternative sources of news. The news media have considerable impact on what we know, and they need to realize the impact that their work has on the lives of the American public, and report the news as accurately, completely, and objectively as they can, for the good of the people. A communitarian ethic based on Deni Elliott's principles and John Dewey's theory of the opposition of duty and interest would be a good start.

Works Cited

Armao, R. (2000). The history of investigative reporting. In M. Greenwald & J. Bernt (Eds.), The big chill: Investigative reporting in the current media environment (pp. 35–49). Ames, Iowa: Iowa State University Press.

Bergman, L. (2000). Network television news: With fear and favor. *Columbia Journalism Review*, 1, 50–51.

Christians, C. G., Ferré, J. P., & Fackler, P. M. (1993). Good news: Social ethics & the press. New York: Oxford University Press.

Dewey, J. (1916). Democracy and Education. New York: The Macmillan Company.

Edge, M. (2000). And "the wall" came tumbling down. In M. Greenwald & J. Bernt (Eds.), The big chill: Investigative reporting in the current media environment (pp. 197–210). Ames, Iowa: Iowa State University Press.

Ehrlich, M. C. (1995). The competitive ethos in television newswork. *Critical Studies in Mass Communication*, 12, 196.

Goldstein, T. (1999). Does big mean bad? In B. Levy & D. M. Bonilla (Eds.), The power of the press (pp. 24–27). New York: The H. W. Wilson Company.

Guensburg, C. (1998). When the story is about the owner. *American Journalism Review*, 10, 10–11.

Hulteng, J. L. (1985). The messenger's motives. Englewood Cliffs, NJ: Prentice-Hall, Inc.

Idsvoog, K. (1994). TV sitting on stories to improve ratings. Nieman Reports, 1, 38.

Jensen, C. (1996). Censored: The news that didn't make the news and why. New York: Seven Stories Press.

Kirtley, J. (1998). Second-guessing news judgment. *American Journalism Review*, 20, 86.

Krajicek, D. J. (1998). Scooped! Media miss real story on crime while chasing sex, sleaze, and celebrities. New York: Columbia University Press.

McCartney, J. (1997). News lite. In B. Levy & D. M. Bonilla (Eds.), The power of the press (pp. 44–54). New York: The H. W. Wilson Company.

Trigoboff, D. (2000, August 28). Reporter wins in milk suit. *Broadcasting & Cable*, 130, 27.

Winch, S. P. (2000). Ethical challenges for investigative journalism. In M. Greenwald & J. Bernt (Eds.), The big chill: Investigative reporting in the current media environment (pp. 121–136). Ames, Iowa: Iowa State University Press.

2

Social Media Has Changed Journalism for the Better

Andrea Carson

Andrea Carson lectures on media matters at La Trobe University, a school in Australia. Her latest book is an academic title, published by Routledge, called Investigative Journalism, Democracy and the Digital Age.

While more popular applications of social media involve video games and memes, Andrea Carson is optimistic about the possibility those platforms also promise journalists around the world. In pursuit of their stories, reporters now have the capacity to speak to almost anyone, and conversely, almost anyone can be a reporter. In this way, the kinds of stories being written today differ from their geographically constrained ancestors and, Carson believes, come closer to the truth.

Borrowing Malcolm Turnbull's election slogan, optimists would say there has never been a more exciting time to be a journalist. Why? Part of the answer lies with social media and the digital age.

A recent trip to Nepal for the second Asian investigative journalism conference revealed something exciting is changing journalism. In a digital era that promotes sharing through tweets,

"How Investigative Journalists Are Using Social Media to Uncover the Truth," by Andrea Carson, The Conversation, October 18, 2016. https://theconversation.com/how-investigative-journalists-are-using-social-media-to-uncover-the-truth-66393. Licensed under CC BY-ND 4.0.

likes and follows, reporters are sharing too—not just their own stories, but also their skills.

They no longer view each other as simply rivals competing for a scoop, but collaborators who can share knowledge to expose wrongdoing for the public good.

Take, for example, the Panama Papers that broke in April this year. It involved almost 400 journalists together trawling through 11.5 million leaked documents from law firm Mossack Fonseca to expose the shady global industry of secret tax havens.

Another version of this type of collaboration occurred in Kathmandu last month. Eighty of the world's best investigative journalists from the *New York Times*, the *Guardian* and other quality outlets met to train hundreds of reporters from across the globe in digital journalism. Classes included data reporting, mapping and visualisations, online searching, tracking dirty money, co-ordinating cross-border reporting teams and effective use of social media.

The Global Investigative Journalism Network (GIJN) chose Nepal as the host country so that journalists from less-developed economies—many with limited political and civil freedoms—could attend to learn how to strengthen watchdog reporting in their home countries.

Reporting in these nations can be difficult, and some stories told were horrific. Umar Cheema, a Panama Papers reporter and investigative journalist for Pakistan's the *News International*, described how he was abducted by unknown assailants in 2010, stripped, shaved and beaten. His "crime" was to report critically on the Pakistani government, intelligence services and military.

His captors have not been caught. But rather than remain silent, he shared his story with the world and was awarded the Daniel Pearl Fellowship to work at the *New York Times* in 2008.

Despite diverse backgrounds with varying levels of press freedom, journalists came to Kathmandu with the same motive: to give voice to the powerless against those who abuse power; whether it be corrupt governments, corporations or individuals.

Unique to the digital age, this can be achieved with tools as simple as a mobile phone and internet connection. Social media platforms are useful too, to distribute stories beyond the territories that oppress them.

Among the watchdog journalism educators were Pulitzer Prize winners, including Walter "Robbie" Robinson. Now editor-at-large at the *Boston Globe*, Robinson is the reporter played by Michael Keaton in this year's Oscar winner for Best Picture, *Spotlight*.

The film tells how Robinson in 2001 led the Spotlight team's investigation that uncovered widespread sexual abuse in the Catholic Church. That investigation inspired other journalists around the world to probe and eventually expose the church's widespread abuses of power. Robinson's message was simple:

> *To me you are all Spotlight reporters. For the great journalism you have done and will do. For your energy, for your passion, for your courage, for your tenacity, for your commitment to righting wrong and for knowing with a certainty, that there is no injustice however grave that cannot be eradicated by those who unearth the truth.*

To unearth truths, trainers profiled free digital search tools like Picodash for trawling Instagram, and Amnesty International's YouTube DataViewer, as well as reverse image searching programs like TinEye.

Thomson Reuters' Data editor Irene Liu showed reporters how to search for people using Pipl, ways to navigate blog content using Kinja, and creative techniques to search social media. Sites like Twitter, Facebook and LinkedIn can be trawled using Rapportive and Chrome extension Storyful Multisearch to find public interest information quickly and cheaply.

Here are five ways that social media is changing journalism in the digital age:

1. Reach: social media offers journalism a potential global playing field. It is used for sharing stories but also crowdsourcing information and enabling local stories of

significance to spread beyond geographical boundaries. Whether it is the Arab Spring uprising or the recent hurricane in Haiti, journalists can source contacts and share stories with the rest of the world.
2. Participation: social media provides a many-to-many network that allows for audience participation and interaction. It provides for audience comment, and these interactions can take the story forward.
3. Hyperlocal reporting: social media is filling a gap in hyperlocal reporting. In a recent study we found community groups, including the local police at Broadmeadows, used social media to provide local news. This helped fill a reporting hole left by the shrinking newsrooms of local newspapers.
4. Low cost: social media is a fast and cheap way to find, produce and share news. It lowers the barriers to entry for start-up news outlets and freelance journalists.
5. Independence: journalists can bypass state-controlled media and other limits on publishing their stories. They can report independently without editorial interference, and broadcast their own movements, using publicity for self-protection.

The benefits social media can offer journalism, particularly in developing economies, is not to deny the challenges established media outlets face in developed countries in the digital age.

Certainly, the rise of digital media technologies has fractured the business model of traditional media as advertising has migrated online, causing revenue losses. In turn, these have sparked masses of newsroom job losses, cutbacks, and masthead closures.

But for all the pervasive pessimism about the future of established news outlets, and the negative aspects of social media such as trolling, the Nepal conference demonstrated the positives as well.

Digital tools are changing the ways in which journalists find, tell and share their stories with audiences beyond the control of state borders. Yet, at the same time, new technologies enable journalists to do what they have always done: to uncover stories in the public interest.

Giuseppe Tomasi di Lampedusa wrote in *The Leopard*:

If we want things to stay as they are, things will have to change.

So it is with journalism in the digital age.

3

Snowden's Whistleblowing Prompted Public Awareness
Ewen MacAskill and Alex Hern

Ewen MacAskill is a military and intelligence reporter, most notable for his work at the Guardian, *where he helped produce its Pulitzer Prize–winning reporting on documents that had been leaked by Edward Snowden. Alex Hern is a technology reporter at the newspaper.*

In the early 2010s, Edward Snowden was a household name. As a disillusioned security consultant for a contractor employed by the National Security Agency, he revealed the existence of a massive telephone metadata surveillance system. The story won that year's Pulitzer Prize and was made by Laura Poitras into an Oscar-winning documentary called Citizenfour. *It also was dramatized by Oliver Stone and Joseph Gordon-Levitt into a movie, simply called* Snowden. *Here, one of the reporters involved in that story talks to Edward Snowden himself about what he thinks the impact of that story has been on society. The most important change, he tells the* Guardian's *Ewen MacAskill, was public awareness.*

Edward Snowden has no regrets five years on from leaking the biggest cache of top-secret documents in history. He is wanted by the US. He is in exile in Russia. But he is satisfied with the way

"Edward Snowden: 'The People Are Still Powerless, but Now They're Aware,'" by Ewen MacAskill and Alex Hern, Guardian News & Media Limited, June 4, 2018. Reprinted by permission.

his revelations of mass surveillance have rocked governments, intelligence agencies and major internet companies.

In a phone interview to mark the anniversary of the day the *Guardian* broke the story, he recalled the day his world—and that of many others around the globe—changed for good. He went to sleep in his Hong Kong hotel room and when he woke, the news that the National Security Agency had been vacuuming up the phone data of millions of Americans had been live for several hours.

Snowden knew at that moment his old life was over. "It was scary but it was liberating," he said. "There was a sense of finality. There was no going back."

What has happened in the five years since? He is one of the most famous fugitives in the world, the subject of an Oscar-winning documentary, a Hollywood movie, and at least a dozen books. The US and UK governments, on the basis of his revelations, have faced court challenges to surveillance laws. New legislation has been passed in both countries. The internet companies, responding to a public backlash over privacy, have made encryption commonplace.

Snowden, weighing up the changes, said some privacy campaigners had expressed disappointment with how things have developed, but he did not share it. "People say nothing has changed: that there is still mass surveillance. That is not how you measure change. Look back before 2013 and look at what has happened since. Everything changed."

The most important change, he said, was public awareness. "The government and corporate sector preyed on our ignorance. But now we know. People are aware now. People are still powerless to stop it but we are trying. The revelations made the fight more even."

He said he had no regrets. "If I had wanted to be safe, I would not have left Hawaii [where he had been based, working for the NSA, before flying to Hong Kong]."

His own life is uncertain, perhaps now more than ever, he said. His sanctuary in Russia depends on the whims of the Putin government, and the US and UK intelligence agencies have not forgiven him. For them, the issue is as raw as ever, an act of betrayal they say caused damage on a scale the public does not realise.

This was reflected in a rare statement from Jeremy Fleming, the director of the UK surveillance agency GCHQ, which, along with the US National Security Agency, was the main subject of the leak. In response to a question from the *Guardian* about the anniversary, Fleming said GCHQ's mission was to keep the UK safe: "What Edward Snowden did five years ago was illegal and compromised our ability to do that, causing real and unnecessary damage to the security of the UK and our allies. He should be accountable for that."

The anger in the US and UK intelligence communities is over not just what was published—fewer than 1% of the documents—but extends to the unpublished material too. They say they were forced to work on the assumption everything Snowden ever had access to had been compromised and had to be dumped.

There was a plus for the agencies. Having scrapped so much, they were forced to develop and install new and better capabilities faster than planned. Another change came in the area of transparency. Before Snowden, media requests to GCHQ were usually met with no comment whereas now there is more of a willingness to engage. That Fleming responds with a statement reflects that stepchange.

In his statement, he expressed a commitment to openness but pointedly did not credit Snowden, saying the change predated 2013. "It is important that we continue to be as open as we can be, and I am committed to the journey we began over a decade ago to greater transparency," he said.

Others in the intelligence community, especially in the US, will grudgingly credit Snowden for starting a much-needed debate about where the line should be drawn between privacy and surveillance. The former deputy director of the NSA Richard Ledgett, when retiring last year, said the government should have made public the fact there was bulk collection of phone data.

The former GCHQ director Sir David Omand shared Fleming's assessment of the damage but admitted Snowden had contributed to the introduction of new legislation. "A sounder and more transparent legal framework is now in place for necessary intelligence gathering. That would have happened eventually, of course, but his actions certainly hastened the process," Omand said.

The US Congress passed the Freedom Act in 2015, curbing the mass collection of phone data. The UK parliament passed the contentious Investigatory Powers Act a year later.

Ross Anderson, a leading academic specialising in cybersecurity and privacy, sees the Snowden revelations as a seminal moment. Anderson, a professor of security engineering at Cambridge University's computer laboratory, said: "Snowden's revelations are one of these flashbulb moments which change the way people look at things. They may not have changed things much in Britain because of our culture for adoring James Bond and all his works. But round the world it brought home to everyone that surveillance really is an issue."

MPs and much of the UK media did not engage to the same extent of their counterparts elsewhere in Europe, the US, Latin America, Asia and Australia. Among the exceptions was the Liberal Democrat MP Julian Huppert, who pressed the issue until he lost his seat in 2015. "The Snowden revelations were a huge shock but they have led to a much greater transparency from some of the agencies about the sort of the things they were doing," he said.

One of the disclosures to have most impact was around the extent of collaboration between the intelligence agencies and internet companies. In 2013, the US companies were outsmarting the EU in negotiations over data protection. Snowden landed like a bomb in the middle of the negotiations and the data protection law that took effect last month is a consequence.

One of the most visible effects of the Snowden revelations was the small yellow bubble that began popping up on the messaging service WhatsApp in April 2016: "Messages to this chat and calls are now secured with end-to-end encryption."

Before Snowden, such encryption was for the targeted and the paranoid. "If I can take myself back to 2013," said Jillian York, the director for international freedom of expression at the digital rights group the Electronic Frontier Foundation, "I maybe had the precursor to [the encrypted communication app] Signal on my phone, TextSecure. I had [another email encryption tool] PGP, but nobody used it." The only major exception was Apple's iMessage, which has been end-to-end encrypted since it was launched in 2011.

Developers at major technology companies, outraged by the Snowden disclosures, started pushing back. Some, such as those at WhatsApp, which was bought by Facebook a year after the story broke, implemented their own encryption. Others, such as Yahoo's Alex Stamos, quit rather than support further eavesdropping. (Stamos is now the head of security at Facebook.)

"Without Snowden," said York, "I don't think Signal would have got the funding. I don't think Facebook would have had Alex Stamos, because he would have been at Yahoo. These little things led to big things. It's not like all these companies were like "we care about privacy. I think they were pushed."

Other shifts in the technology sector show Snowden's influence has in many ways been limited. The rise of the "smart speaker," exemplified by Amazon's Echo, has left many privacy activists baffled. Why, just a few years after a global scandal involving government surveillance, would people willingly install always-on microphones in their homes?

"The new-found privacy conundrum presented by installing a device that can literally listen to everything you're saying represents a chilling new development in the age of internet-connected things," wrote Gizmodo's Adam Clark Estes last year.

Towards the end of the interview, Snowden recalled one of his early aliases, Cincinnatus, after the Roman who after public service returned to his farm. Snowden said he too felt that, having played his role, he had retreated to a quieter life, spending time developing tools to help journalists protect their sources. "I do not think I have ever been more fulfilled," he said.

But he will not be marking the anniversary with a "victory lap," he said. There is still much to be done. "The fightback is just beginning," said Snowden. "The governments and the corporates have been in this game a long time and we are just getting started."

4

The Public Wants Unbiased News

Amy Mitchell, Katie Simmons, Katerina Eva Matsa, and Laura Silver

Amy Mitchell, Katie Simmons, Katerina Eva Matsa, and Laura Silver are writers at the Pew Research Center, a nonpartisan think tank based in Washington, DC.

A recent survey by the Pew Research Center suggests that most people yearn, on some level, for media that reads as unbiased but that they are, also, perpetually unsatisfied, and their dissatisfaction stems largely from their own political views. The most arresting revelation in the Pew study, for instance, is that conservatives in the United States say that they feel unsatisfied with news coverage even when their political party dominates the halls of power. This suggests feeling alienated from the "media" may be, itself, an inherently political position.

Publics around the world overwhelmingly agree that the news media should be unbiased in their coverage of political issues, according to a new Pew Research Center survey of 38 countries. Yet, when asked how their news media are doing on reporting different political issues fairly, people are far more mixed in their sentiments, with many saying their media do not deliver. And, in many countries, there are sharp political differences in views of the media—with the largest gap among Americans.

"Publics Globally Want Unbiased News Coverage, but Are Divided on Whether Their News Media Deliver," by Amy Mitchell, Katie Simmons, Katerina Eva Matsa, and Laura Silver, Pew Research Center, January 11, 2018.

To build off Pew Research Center's earlier findings about US news media habits and attitudes, this new cross-national survey begins to study these dynamics globally. The survey finds that a median of 75% across 38 countries say it is never acceptable for a news organization to favor one political party over others when reporting the news. Just 20% say this is sometimes okay. People in Europe show the greatest opposition to political bias in their news, including 89% in Spain and 88% in Greece who think this is unacceptable. In the United States, 78% say the news media should never favor one political party over another. In only five countries do at least three-in-ten believe it is okay to favor one side.

While publics around the globe place a premium on politically unbiased news media, this is precisely the performance area, among four asked about, where publics are least likely to say their news media are doing well. A median of only 52% across the 38 nations polled say the news media in their country do a good job of reporting on political issues fairly, while 44% say they do not. And although majorities of the public in 18 countries say their news media are performing well in this area, attitudes are more negative in the remaining 20 nations surveyed. The most critical are Spain, Greece, South Korea, Lebanon and Chile, where at least six-in-ten say their news media do not do well on reporting the news fairly.

News media receive considerably higher marks in other performance areas. Broad majorities say their news media do a good job of covering the most important stories (median of 73%), reporting the news accurately (62%), and reporting news about government leaders and officials (59%). People in sub-Saharan Africa and the Asia-Pacific are more satisfied with their news media, while Latin Americans are the most critical. The US public tends to fall roughly in the middle across the different performance areas asked about.

Within countries, political identification tends to be the strongest divider of media attitudes, more so than education, age or gender.

Political party systems vary considerably across countries, but one consistent measure for comparing political divides is support for the governing party or parties. Individuals who identify with the governing party or parties are categorized as supporters, everyone else as nonsupporters. In the US, this means that people who identify with the Republican Party, which currently controls all branches of the federal government, are considered governing party supporters. People who identify with the Democratic Party, say they are independent, identify with some other party or do not identify with any political party are categorized as nonsupporters.

Using this approach, large gaps in ratings of the media emerge between governing party supporters and nonsupporters. On the question of whether their news media cover political issues fairly, for example, partisan differences appear in 20 of the 38 countries surveyed. In five countries, the gap is at least 20 percentage points, with the largest by far in the US at 34 percentage points. The next highest partisan gap is in Israel, with a 26-point difference.

The US is also one of only a few countries where governing party supporters are less satisfied with their news media than are nonsupporters. In most countries, people who support the political party currently in power are more satisfied with the performance of their news media than those who do not support the governing party. For example, in Sweden, the Social Democratic Party and the Green Party are the two parties that currently form the governing coalition in the country. About eight-in-ten Swedes (82%) who identify with these two parties say their news media do a good job of covering political issues fairly. Just 58% of Swedes who do not identify with these two parties agree.

The partisan gaps found in the survey indicate that, rather than being consistently tied to a particular ideological position, satisfaction with the news media across the globe is more closely related to support for the party in power—whether that party is left or right. Public satisfaction with the news media also links closely to trust in one's national government and a sense that the economy is doing well, which reinforces the point that, for most countries surveyed here, satisfaction with the media aligns with satisfaction on other country conditions rather than along a left-right spectrum.

These are among the major findings of a Pew Research Center survey conducted among 41,953 respondents in 38 countries from Feb. 16 to May 8, 2017. In addition to the topics discussed above, the study also focuses on individuals' use of the internet and social media to get news, as well as the types of news people follow.

Online News Is Making Inroads in Many Countries Around the World

Digital technology is influencing news habits across the globe, though its use is still far from universal. Overall, a median of 42% among the 38 countries surveyed say they get news on the internet at least once a day. In 14 countries, half or more adults get news online daily.

In general, internet access has been shown to be higher in wealthier countries, and this plays out to a greater likelihood of using the internet for news as well. For example, 61% in Australia—which had a 2015 gross domestic product (GDP) per capita of $46,271—get news at least once a day through the internet. Just 20% in Senegal, with a GDP per capita of $2,421, do the same.

The survey also asked a separate question about how often people get news specifically on social media sites. Unlike getting news on the internet generally, the percentage that gets news on social media is not strongly related to country wealth. In fact, the median percentages of people who get news at least once a day through social media are about the same in emerging and developing economies as in advanced ones (33% and 36%, respectively). Overall, a global median of 35% get news daily through social media, with the highest levels in South Korea (57%), Lebanon (52%) and Argentina (51%).

Public Is Highly Engaged with News, but More So with News That's Close to Home

Overall interest in the news has implications for how news media landscapes develop alongside technological change. Large majorities around the world say they follow national and local news closely (global medians of 86% and 78% respectively). In all 38 countries, more than two-thirds say this of news about their own country. The same is true of news about their city or town in 32 countries.

People are much less interested in news about other countries (global median of 57%). In only six countries do more than two-thirds say they pay close attention to news about the rest of the world. People outside of the US express a similarly low level of interest in news specifically about the US (48%).

Young More Likely to Get News Online; Older People More Likely to Follow the News Overall

Across all 38 countries, young people—those ages 18 to 29—are more likely to get news online than adults 50 and older. In 11 countries, the age gap is 35 percentage points or greater.

At the same time, older people tend to be more interested in the various types of news asked about than the younger generation. The biggest gaps are in news about one's own city or town. In 20 countries, people ages 50 and older are significantly more likely than people younger than 30 to closely follow local news. The age gap is at least 15 percentage points in 11 of the countries. Only in the Philippines and Brazil is the pattern reversed; there, young people are more likely to follow local news.

For international news, age is less of a factor. In general, men and those with more education are more likely to follow international news.

5

The Media Feedback Loop
Jonathan Stray

Jonathan Stray is a computer scientist and a freelance journalist who taught computational journalism at Columbia University. These days, he's a fellow at Partnership on AI, a nonprofit that works with artificial intelligence.

In most countries, national elections are among the most widely reported events; in the United States, presidential elections are presented as multi-year-long press sagas that culminate in an all-night, televised wait for the results. It's hard to say that this is, necessarily, a bad thing. Mass participation is central to the idea of a democracy, and the reporting that these cycles generate is what gives voters the information that informs the decisions they make in the ballot box. But Jonathan Stray looks at the 2016 election and wonders if the press coverage itself sways elections. Donald Trump, a businessman and TV personality, handily managed to accrue more media coverage than any of his rivals. Did this contribute to his win?

Whether your favorite candidate is popular or unpopular, it's always popular to blame the media. We see a lot of this right now in discussions of why Trump is in the lead or why Sanders isn't.

"How Much Influence Does the Media Really Have over Elections? Digging into the Data," by Jonathan Stray, President and Fellow of Harvard College, January 11, 2016. Reprinted by permission. Published by arrangement with the Nieman Foundation for Journalism.

Usually the complaints have to do with what the media is saying about a candidate. But another theory says that it's the attention that matters. Good news or bad—maybe the important thing is just to be talked about.

Or maybe professional journalists have very little influence at all. Many people now get their news by clicking on articles from social media, where your friends and a filtering algorithm decide what you see.

So does the media still matter? Does attention get results for candidates, regardless of what is said? And if it does, how should journalists cover elections fairly and responsibly? These are the questions I wanted to try to answer, at least as they relate the current US presidential primaries.

Attention vs. Popularity

These are big questions about how the American political system works, far too big for simple answers. But you have to start somewhere, so I decided to compare the number of times each 2016 candidate has been mentioned in the US mainstream media with their standing in national primary polls. To my surprise, the two line up almost exactly.

This chart [not shown] shows the number of times a candidate's full name appeared in the top 25 online news sources, as a percentage of all mentions, for October to December of 2015. (Republican candidates were mentioned about twice as often as Democratic candidates overall, but this chart compares each candidate to the others within their party.) There's an uncanny agreement between the media attention and each candidate's standing in national primary polls. It's a textbook correlation.

Depending on what corner of the political universe you come from, it may surprise you to learn that both Trump and Sanders were covered in proportion to their poll results—at least online. Pretty much everyone was. The exceptions are Jeb Bush, who seems to have been covered twice as much as his standing would suggest, and Carson, who might have been slightly under-covered.

By simply counting the number of mentions, we're completely ignoring what journalists are actually saying, including whether the coverage was positive or negative. This data doesn't say anything at all about tone or frame or even what issues were discussed. All of these things might be very important in the larger context of democracy, but they seem to be less important in terms of primary poll results. While the story surely matters, it doesn't seem to matter as much as the attention. In particular, Trump has received much more negative coverage than his GOP competitors, to little apparent effect.

I admit I was a bit shocked to discover how closely the percentage of media mentions and the percentage of voter support align. But I'm also not the first to notice. Nate Silver found that this pattern holds in US primary elections going back to 1980, though his model also incorporated favorability ratings. This correlation has also been noticed by previous political science researchers, though I haven't been able to find anywhere it's been seriously investigated.

So what's going on here? How do all the numbers on this chart just line up? Does this mean the media exert near-total control over the political process? Fortunately, no. To begin with, national primary polls don't predict the eventual nominee very well; state polls matter much more, because the nominating process happens one state at a time. But it seems reasonable to imagine that media attention has some effect on the polls. Yet journalists also respond to the polls, which means it isn't clear what's causing what.

Which Came First: The Media or the Polls?

If you're worried about the media's influence you're thinking of a causal relationship like this: media attention drives poll results.

But there are two other ways that these variables can become highly correlated. First, causality could go the other way. The polls could drive the media.

This isn't completely insane. Journalists have to follow audience attention or risk getting ignored. And if voters are also readers, a candidate who is twice as popular might get twice the number of views and shares. That matters when you're deciding what to cover—though it's hardly the only consideration. More on that later.

There's one more way to get a close relationship between media and polls: something else could be driving both of them. For example, attention on social media could drive both. A single post can go viral and reach millions without any involvement from professional journalists.

Or perhaps endorsements from famous people and organizations are the key to influence, as political scientists have long suspected. And then there are the candidates themselves: anything they do might make them more (or less!) favorable with both the media and the public. In short we need to consider every other thing, and many of these things will drive media attention and voter preference in the same direction, causing a correlation like the one we've seen.

These are the basic causal forces, the only possible ways that media attention and polling results can become so closely aligned. We're going to need more information to figure out what is causing what.

One way to test for causality is to ask whether a change in coverage precedes a change in the polls, or vice versa. [For example, a comparison of] the number of articles mentioning the right-wing UK Independence Party (UKIP) versus poll results, tracked over 11 years in the British press.

[A] chart by James Murphy of Southhampton University, [shows] changes across time, rather than between parties. Yet once again, coverage and popularity follow each other closely. To determine which came first, Murphy built a statistical model that tries to predict this month's polls from the previous month's coverage, and vice versa. Whichever direction works better, that's the way the cause runs. But the results were inconclusive—they depended on exactly how the model was put together. This suggests that the causality goes both ways.

[A] similar chart of popularity and coverage over time for Trump [shows that] Trump's polls and mentions rose at about the same rate after he announced his candidacy, so at first glance it looks like the two are tied together. But media spikes don't always translate into polling spikes: Both debates produced a spike in coverage, but the polls actually decreased in the short term. The burst of coverage after he announced his plan to exclude Muslims does seem to line up with a bump in popularity, though.

John Sides of George Washington University has done a statistical analysis to try to tease out the causality in Trump's data and, once again, the results don't clearly favor the chicken or the egg. Instead, it seems that the media and the polls drive each other loosely. Most of the other candidates show the same general pattern.

We typically see a rise after the candidate announcement, then general agreement with the level of media coverage even though the peaks don't line up. Clinton seems to be the exception: Her popularity seems to have less to do with coverage volume than any other candidate. Maybe that's because we've known for a very long time that she was going to run, and we should really plot this chart back another year or two.

My sense is that what we have here is a feedback loop. Does media attention increase a candidate's standing in the polls? Yes. Does a candidate's standing in the polls increase media attention? Also yes. And everything else that sways both journalists and voters in the same direction just increases the correlation. The media and the public and the candidates are embedded in a system where every part affects every other.

It's all of these forces acting in concert that tend to bind media attention and popularity together. It's not that media attention has no effect—we have good reason to believe it does, both from this data and from other research. It's just that the media is not all powerful, despite what the close correlation suggests.

What Is Fair Election Coverage?

Faced with the awesome ability to influence the outcome of an election just by drawing attention to a candidate, how should the media cover an election?

No editor is sitting there saying: Hey, Cruz gained five points, let's cover him 5 percent more. But journalists do respond to audience attention. Reporters and editors are driven by lots of different demand signals, such as how many people read yesterday's article about a candidate, or how many people are talking about a candidate on social media or—let's be honest here—how popular someone seems to be based on how much coverage they are getting from other journalists! Some newsrooms even plan coverage based on how many people are searching for a given topic.

The media is regularly criticized for chasing popularity, and in this sense it's true. Bernie Sanders says the "corporate media" trivialize the issues and only care about profits. There is certainly no profit without readers—there's no funding either, if you're a nonprofit newsroom. The rapper Common says "the integrity of the media is gone" when journalists decide "we're going to show Donald Trump because we know it's about numbers." And these complaints are not wrong. I began writing this piece to explore the media's relationship to Trump in part because I knew a piece about Trump was likely to be widely read!

Yet for all the newsroom profit pressure and manic metric checking, journalists don't only chase popularity. The American media cover a great many things that few people pay attention to, especially international stories. For example, there was extensive coverage of bombings in Lebanon a day before the Paris attacks, despite complaints to the contrary. There's an ongoing, thoughtful conversation among journalists about how to balance what gets clicks with what's important. That is, what journalists think is important. I'll say this for writing what the audience wants to read: It's democratic.

So should a candidate get media attention according to how many people want to read about them? On some level, yes. But if you think Trump shouldn't be leading or Sanders should be, this probably doesn't seem fair to you. To the degree that media attention causes a candidate to become more popular, there's a winner-take-all effect here: The leading candidate will get the most coverage, boosting their lead. Meanwhile, the media has the potential to trap a candidate in last place because they can't get the coverage they would need in order to rise in the polls.

But what's the alternative? Should journalists cover every candidate equally? This might make a certain amount of sense in the general election, where we only have two major parties. The FCC still enforces the equal time rule, which says that if a radio or TV network gives one candidate airtime, they have to give the same amount to other candidates. But that rule doesn't apply to news programs, and that's probably for the best. It's ridiculous to imagine journalists struggling to reach story quotas, so that each candidate gets the same amount of press.

But if not equal time, should journalists strive for some other redistribution of attention? This would necessarily mean less coverage for the leaders and more for everyone else. This might lead to more competitive elections, in that it would counter the winner-take-all tendency of the current system. But it would also mean intentionally not covering Trump as much. This might balance things out in an abstract sort of way, but it would also open the media to charges of censorship—and those charges would not be without merit.

It also won't work to suggest the press should just report "current events" or whatever is "newsworthy," as if the news makes itself. Journalism has become less and less about events over the last 50 years, and more and more about context and analysis. And that's okay: Politicians and brands are their own media channels now. If all you want to know is what a candidate did today, you can just follow them on social media—no need for professional journalists at all. Journalists have to add value in other ways now, such as providing context or digging deeper. There's no obviously "right" number of stories about a candidate.

The Media's Influence on Society

Somewhere, somehow, professional journalists have to decide who gets covered—and any formula they could choose is going to appear biased to someone. In the end, the candidates who attack the media are right about one thing: The press is a political player in its own right. There's just no way to avoid that when attention is valuable.

6

Media Reform Is Essential to Democracy
Robert W. McChesney

Robert W. McChesney is a professor of communication at the University of Illinois at Urbana–Champaign and cofounder of Free Press, a special interest group that lobbies for net neutrality, among other issues.

Writing shortly after the passing of the Telecommunications Act of 1996, Robert McChesney bemoans the rapid consolidation of media properties that quickly followed and persists today. In "noncompetitive markets" like local broadcast news, massive corporations like the Sinclair Broadcast Group, which has quietly amassed 193 such stations, have dominated. The impact of this consolidation is fundamentally corrosive, McChesney argues in this excerpted viewpoint. In its place, he advocates for a public-private system not unlike that of the United Kingdom, where a government-owned broadcaster like the BBC would set a noncommercial tone that the rest of the media marketplace would follow.

The case for media reform is based on two propositions. First, *media perform essential political, social, economic, and cultural functions in modern democracies*. In such societies, media are the principal source of political information and access to public debate, and the key to an informed, participating, self-governing citizenry. Democracy requires a media system that provides people

"Making Media Democratic," by Robert W. McChesney, *Boston Review*. Reprinted by permission.

with a wide range of opinion and analysis and debate on important issues, reflects the diversity of citizens, and promotes public accountability of the powers-that-be and the powers-that-want-to-be. In short, the media in a democracy must foster deliberation and diversity, and ensure accountability.

Second, *media organization—patterns of ownership, management, regulation, and subsidy—is a central determinant of media content*. This proposition is familiar from discussions of media in China and the former Soviet Union. For those countries, the idea that the media could promote deliberation, diversity, and accountability, while being effectively owned and controlled by the Communist Party, was not even worth refuting. Similarly, we are not surprised to hear that when cronies of the Mexican government owned the country's only TV station, television news coverage was especially favorable to the ruling party.

[…]

In such noncompetitive markets, the claim that media firms "give the people what they want" is unconvincing. The firms have enough market power to dictate the content that is most profitable for them. And the easy route to profit comes from increasing commercialism— larger numbers of ads, greater say for advertisers over non-advertising content, programming that lends itself to merchandising, and all sorts of cross promotions with non-media firms. Consumers may not want such hyper-commercialism, but they have little say in the matter. So we have a 50 percent increase in the number of commercials on network TV in the past decade; the development of commercially-saturated kids' programming as arguably the fastest-growing and most profitable branch of the TV industry in the 1990s; becoming standard in motion pictures. The flip side of this commercialism is the decline of public service—of the notion that there is any purpose to our media except to make money for shareholders.

Under such conditions, journalistic norms can hardly be expected to stem the commercial tide. Contemporary commercial journalism is essentially a mix of crime stories, celebrity profiles, consumer news pitched at the upper middle class, and warmed over press releases. Bookstores are filled with dispirited reports by former editors and journalists bemoaning the brave new world of corporate journalism. Journalist unions are very important in this regard, by protecting journalistic norms from the commercial interests of the owners. But without other measures to weaken corporate media power, unions are not likely to be able to resist pressures from the current media system.

For democrats, then, media competition and journalistic norms do not suffice for deliberation, diversity, and accountability. If media are central to the formation of a participating and informed citizenry, and if media organization influences media performance, then issues about ownership, regulation, and subsidy need to be matters of public debate. But such debate has been almost non-existent in the United States. Even in broadcasting, where the publicly owned airwaves are licensed to private users, the public has never had any meaningful participation in the formation of policy.

Consider the Telecommunications Act of 1996. The law it replaced, the Communications Act of 1934, regulated telephony, radio, and television. The 1996 Act provides the basis for determining the course of radio, television, telephony, the Internet—indeed virtually all aspects of communication as we shift over to digital technologies. Its guiding premise is that the market should rule communication, with government assistance. The politics of the Act consisted largely of powerful corporate communication firms and lobbies fighting behind the scenes to get the most favorable wording. That the corporate sector would control all communication was a given; the only fight was over which sectors and which firms would get the best deals. The public was for the most part unaware of these debates. The drafting and struggles over the Telecommunications Act of 1996 were hardly discussed in the news media, except in the business and trade press, where the legislation was covered as a story of importance to investors and managers, not citizens, or even consumers.

The results of the Telecommunications Act, with its relaxation of ownership restrictions to promote competition across sectors, have been little short of disastrous. Rather than produce competition, a far-fetched notion in view of the concentrated nature of these markets, the law has paved the way for the greatest period of corporate concentration in US media and communication history.

[…]

[Some] reformers have turned to "civic" or "public" journalism, a well-intentioned attempt to reduce the sensationalism and blatant political manipulation of mainstream journalism. Unfortunately, the movement completely ignores the structural factors of ownership and advertising that have led to the attack on journalism. Public journalism, not surprisingly, is averse to "ideological" approaches to the news, and therefore encourages a boringly "balanced" and soporific newsfare. Claiming to give readers news they think is important to their lives, advocates of public journalism may in fact be assisting in the process of converting journalism into the type of consumer news and information that delights the advertising community.

Still others have joined the media literacy movement. The idea here is to educate people to be skeptical and knowledgeable users of the media. Media literacy has considerable potential so long as it involves explaining how the media system actually works, and leads people to work for a better system. But a more conventional wing of the movement implicitly accepts that commercial media "give the people what they want." So the media literacy crowd's job is to train people to demand better fare. The resulting strategy may simply help to prop up the existing system. "Hey, don't blame us for the lousy stuff we provide," the corporate media giants will say. "We even bankrolled media literacy to train people to demand higher quality fare. The morons simply demanded more of what we are already doing."

While media literacy has an important role to play in media reform, civic journalism has been at best a mixed blessing. Some observers credit civic journalism, which is widespread in North Carolina, with helping in Jesse Helms's 1996 re-election. Why? Because civic journalism was ill-equipped to generate tough questions, or press politicians to answer them. So Helms got a cakewalk from the press, barely having to defend his record.

The evidence is clear: if we want a media system that produces fundamentally different results, we need solutions that address the causes of the problems; have to address issues of media ownership, management, regulation, and subsidy. Our goal should be to craft a media system that reduces the power of a handful of enormous corporations and advertisers to dominate the media culture. But no one will press for reform until we have some ideas worth debating. The ultimate trump card of the status quo is the claim that any change in our media system will invariably lead to darkness at noon.

[…]

Media Reform Proposals

Public Broadcasting: Establishing a strong nonprofit sector to complement the commercial giants is not enough. The costs of creating a more democratic media system simply are too high. Therefore, it is important to establish and maintain a noncommercial, nonprofit, public radio and television system. The system should include national networks, local stations, public access television, and independent community radio stations. Every community should also have a stratum of low-power television and micropower radio stations.

The United States has never experienced public broadcasting in the manner of Japan, Canada, and Western Europe. In contrast to the US, public broadcasting there has been well funded and commissioned to serve the entire population. In the United States, public broadcasting has always been underfunded, and effectively required to provide only programming that is not commercially viable. As a result, public broadcasters typically provide relatively unattractive programming to fringe audiences, hardly a strategy for institutional success. Moreover, Congress has been a watchdog to see that public broadcasting did not expand the range of ideological discourse beyond that provided by the commercial broadcasters. In sum, public broadcasting in the United States has been handcuffed since its inception. Still, it has developed a devoted following. This following has provided enough vocal political support to keep US public broadcasting from being effectively privatized, but most of this toothpaste is now out of the tube. Public radio and television are increasingly dependent upon corporate grants and "enhanced underwriting," a euphemism for advertising. The federal subsidy only accounts for some 15 percent of public broadcasting revenues. Indeed, public broadcasting, by the standard international definition, no longer exists in the United States. Instead, we have nonprofit commercial broadcasting, closely linked to the corporate sector, with the constant threat of right-wing political harassment if public stations step out of line.

We need a system of real public broadcasting, with no advertising, that accepts no grants from corporations or private bodies, and that serves the entire population, not merely those who are disaffected from the dominant commercial system and have to contribute during pledge drives. Two hurdles stand in the way of such a system. The first is organizational: How can public broadcasting be structured to make the system accountable and prevent a bureaucracy impervious to popular tastes and wishes, but to give the public broadcasters enough institutional strength to prevent implicit and explicit attempts at censorship by political authorities? The second is fiscal: Where will the funds come from to pay for a viable public broadcasting service? At present, the federal government provides $260 million annually. The public system I envision—which would put per capita US spending in a league with, for example, Britain and Japan—may well cost $5–10 billion annually.

There is no one way to resolve the organizational problem, and perhaps an ideal solution can never be found. But there are better ways, as any comparative survey indicates. One key element in preventing bureaucratic ossification or government meddling will be to establish a pluralistic system, with national networks, local stations, community and public access stations, all controlled independently. In some cases direct election of officers by the public and also by public broadcasting employees may be appropriate, whereas in other cases appointment by elected political bodies may be preferable. As for funding, I have no qualms about drawing the funds for fully public radio and television from general revenues. There is an almost absurd obsession with generating funds for public broadcasting from everywhere but the general budget, on the bogus premise that public broadcasting cannot be justified as a public expense. In view of radio and television's importance in our lives, it clearly deserves a smidgen of the money we use to build entirely unnecessary weapons systems. We subsidize education, but the government now subsidizes media only on behalf of owners. We should seek to have a stable source of funding, one that cannot be subject to manipulation by politicians with little direct interest in the integrity of the system.

A powerful public radio and television system could have a profound effect on our entire media culture. It could lead the way in providing the type of public service journalism that commercialism is now killing off. This might in turn give commercial journalists the impetus they need to pursue the hard stories they now avoid. It could have a similar effect upon our entertainment culture. A viable public TV system could support a legion of small independent filmmakers. It could do wonders for reducing the reliance of our political campaigns upon expensive commercial advertising. It is essential to ensuring the diversity and deliberation that lie at the heart of a democratic public sphere.

Regulation: [Another] main plank is to increase regulation of commercial broadcasting in the public interest. Media reformers have long been active in this arena, if only because the public ownership of the airwaves gives the public, through the FCC, a clear legal right to negotiate terms with the chosen few who get broadcast licenses. Still, even this form of media activism has been negligible, and broadcast regulation has been largely toothless, with the desires of powerful corporations and advertisers rarely challenged.

Experience in the United States and abroad indicates that if commercial broadcasters are not held to high public service standards, they will generate the easiest profits by resorting to the crassest commercialism, and will overwhelm the balance of the media culture. Moreover, standard-setting will not work if commercial broadcasters are permitted to "buy" their way out of public service obligations; the record shows that they will eventually find a way to reduce or eliminate these payments. Hence the most successful mixed system of commercial and public broadcasting in the world was found in Britain from the 1950s to the 1980s. It was successful because the commercial broadcasters were held to public service standards comparable to those employed by the BBC; some scholars even argue that the commercial system sometimes outperformed the BBC as a public service broadcaster. The British scheme worked because commercial broadcasters were threatened with loss of their licenses if they did not meet public service standards. (Regrettably, Thatcherism, with its mantra that the market can do no wrong, has undermined the integrity of the British broadcasting system.)

In three particular areas, broadcast regulation can be of great importance. First, advertising should be strictly regulated or even removed from all children's programming (as in Sweden). We must stop the commercial carpetbombing of our children. Commercial broadcasters should be required to provide several hours per week of ad-free kids' programming, to be produced by artists and educators, not Madison Avenue hotshots.

Second, television news should be taken away from the corporate chiefs and the advertisers and turned over to journalists. Exactly how to organize independent ad-free children's and news programming on commercial television so that it is under the control of educators, artists, and journalists will require study and debate. But we should be able to set up something that is effective.

As for funding this public service programming, I subscribe to the principle that it should be subsidized by the beneficiaries of commercialized communication. This principle might be applied in several ways. We could charge commercial broadcasters rent on the electromagnetic spectrum they use to broadcast. Or we could charge them a tax whenever they sell the stations for a profit. In combination these mechanisms could generate well over a billion dollars annually. Or we could tax advertising. Some $200 billion will be spent to advertise in the United States in 1998, $120 billion of which will be in the media. A very small sales tax on this or even only on that portion that goes to radio and television could generate several billion dollars. It might also have the salutary effect of slowing down the commercial onslaught on American social life. And it does not seem like too much to ask of advertisers who are permitted otherwise to marinate most of the publicly owned spectrum in commercialism.

[…]

Even in these pro-market times, the corporate media have been unable to rid the public of its notion that commercial broadcasters should be required to serve the public as well as shareholders and advertisers. Hence, when commercial broadcasters were able to force the FCC in 1997 to give them (at no cost) massive amounts of new spectrum so they could begin digital TV broadcasting, the Clinton administration established the Gore Commission to recommend public service requirements to be met by broadcasters in return for this gift. Following the contours of US media politics, the Gore Commission has been little short of a farce, with several industry members stonewalling all but the lamest proposals. But we can hope that the Gore Commission will generate some more serious public service proposals, and provide the basis for a public education campaign and subsequent legislation to give them the force of law.

[…]

Not to Worry?

Though the Internet and digital communication in general are certainly creating a radical change in our media and communication systems, the results may not be a more competitive market or more democratic media. Indeed, the evidence to date suggests that as the Internet becomes a commercial medium, the largest media firms are most likely to succeed. The media giants can plug digital programming from their other ventures into the Web at little extra cost. To generate an audience, they can promote their Web sites incessantly on their traditional media holdings. The leading media "brands" have been the first to charge subscription fees for their Web offerings; indeed, they may be the only firms for which this is even an alternative. The media giants can (and do) arrange to have their advertisers agree to advertise on their Web sites. The media giants can also use their market power and brand names to get premier position in Web browser software. The new Microsoft Internet Explorer 4.0 offers 250 highlighted channels, and the "plum positions" belong to Disney and Time Warner. Netscape and Pointcast are making similar arrangements. Moreover, approximately half the venture capital for Internet content start-up companies comes from established media firms; they want to be able to capitalize on profitable new applications as they emerge. In addition, the evidence suggests that in the commercialized Web, advertisers will have increased leverage over content because of the number of choices before them.

[…]

Ironically, the most striking feature of digital communication may well be not that it opened up competition in communication markets, but that it has promoted consolidation by undermining traditional distinctions between radio, television, telecommunication, and computer software. In the 1990s, almost all the media giants have entered into joint ventures or strategic alliances with the largest telecom and software firms. Time Warner is connected to several of the US regional (Bell) telephone giants, as well as to AT&T and Oracle. It has a major joint venture with US West. Disney, likewise, is connected to several major US telecommunication companies, as well as to America Online. News Corp. is partially owned by WorldCom (MCI) and has a joint venture with British Telecom. Microsoft, as one analyst noted, seems to be in bed with everyone. In due course the global media cartel may become something of a global communication cartel.

So how does the rise of the Internet alter my proposals for structural media reform? Very little. There are, of course, some specific policy reforms we should seek for the Internet: for example, guaranteeing universal public access at low rates, perhaps for free, and assuring links for nonprofit Web sites on the dominant browsers and commercial sites. But in general terms, we might do better to regard the Internet as the corporate media giants regard it: as part of the emerging media landscape, not its entirety. So when we create more and smaller media firms, when we create public and community radio and television networks and stations, when we create a strong public service component to commercial news and children's programming, when we use government policies to spawn a nonprofit media sector, all these efforts will have a tremendous effect on the Internet's development as a mass medium. Why? Because Web sites will not be worth much if they do not have the resources to provide a quality product. And all the new media that result from media reform will have Web sites as a mandatory aspect of their operations, much like the commercial media. By creating a vibrant and more democratic "traditional" media culture, we will go a long way toward doing the same with the Web.

Conclusion

Imagine a world in which scores, even hundreds, of media firms operate in markets competitive enough to permit new entrants. Imagine a world with large numbers of public, community, and public access radio and television stations and networks, with enough funding to produce high quality products. Imagine a world where the public airwaves provide compelling journalism, children's programming, and political candidate information, with control vested in people dedicated to public service. Imagine a world where creative government fiscal policies enable small nonprofit and noncommercial media to sprout and prosper, providing some semblance of a democratic public sphere.

Though imaginable, this world seems wholly implausible—and not only because of the political muscle of the corporate media and communications lobbies. Over the past generation, "free market" neoliberals have understood the importance of media as an instrument of social control far better than anyone else. The leading conservative foundations have devoted considerable resources to reducing journalistic autonomy and ideological diversity and pushing media in a more explicitly pro-business direction. The pro-market political right understood that if big business dominated the main fora for political education and debate, then public scrutiny of business would be markedly reduced. These same "free market" foundations fight any public interest component to media laws and regulations, oppose any form of noncommercial and nonprofit media, and lead the battle to ensure that public broadcasting stays within narrow ideological boundaries. In short, we had a major political battle over media for the past generation, but only one side showed up. The results are clear, and appalling.

[…]

Winning major media reform, then, will require the sort of political strength that comes with a broader social movement to democratize our society. We need to see that media reform is a staple of all progressive politics, not just a special interest cause. And media reform may have broad political appeal. Some "cultural conservatives" may be open to calls to reduce the hyper-commercialism of our media culture. And strongly pro-market democrats may recognize that media is an area where the crude application of market principles has produced disastrous "externalities." In sum, the train of media reform is leaving the station. If we value democracy we have no choice but to climb aboard.

7

Investigative Journalism Can Save Lives
Scott Simon

Scott Simon is the host of NPR's Weekend Edition Saturday. *Two-time Pulitzer Prize winner John Carreyrou was a business reporter for the* Wall Street Journal *for two decades.*

Why do massive companies and governments dedicate so much effort to sway the media? One answer might be that they're hiding something. In late 2015, Elizabeth Holmes was trying desperately to kill a story that Wall Street Journal *reporter John Carreyrou was working on about her tech startup, a prospective blood-testing business called Theranos, then valued by investors at $10 billion. Within three years after his story was published, and largely as a consequence of his reporting, the company would be worthless. Here, Carreyrou reflects with NPR's Scott Simon about his pursuit of that story.*

Elizabeth Holmes is—or maybe that should be was—rich, charismatic, and accomplished, the founder and CEO of a company valued at $10 billion that supposedly had developed a device capable of running scores of tests on a tiny, pin-prick drop of blood.

It could have transformed medical care. But earlier this month, Holmes was indicted for wire fraud and conspiracy. The blood test machine her company created doesn't work—and never has. She

---

"Reporter John Carreyrou on the 'Bad Blood' of Theranos," by Scott Simon, National Public Radio, June 23, 2018. Reprinted by permission.

raised almost a billion dollars from investors, including Rupert Murdoch, Carlos Slim Helú, and the family of Betsy DeVos, and signed contracts with Walgreens and Safeway, by lying to them.

John Carreyrou is the *Wall Street Journal* reporter who broke the Theranos story. His new book is *Bad Blood: Secrets and Lies in a Silicon Valley Startup*. He says the big investors Holmes drew in were a combination of ignorant, negligent and foolish. "Walgreens ended up commercializing the technology and offering these faulty blood tests to consumers, not having done its due diligence ... and then the board members and the famous investors, I think, saw that these finger-stick tests were offered in Walgreens stores, and assumed that Walgreens had done its homework."

Interview Highlights

On the Theranos Employees Who Knew Something Was Wrong
You could argue that a lot of people over the years knew that Elizabeth was behaving unethically and overpromising, and that the technology wasn't working. But actually, eventually the reason this whole scandal broke, and that the truth came out, is that a former employee who had been the lab director was willing to talk to me, starting in February of 2015, and it's really thanks to him that this fraud has been exposed.

On Fooling the Press
Ironically, the first publication that put Elizabeth Holmes and Theranos on the map was my own newspaper, the *Wall Street Journal*. She had arranged to be interviewed by an opinion writer ... and that interview took place in August of 2013 and was published right as she went live with the finger-stick tests in Walgreens stores, and unfortunately the writer who wrote that piece, based on the interview, took all her claims at face value. The story that arguably really made her a rock star in Silicon Valley and beyond was the *Fortune* cover story in June of 2014.

On Covering Up the Failure of Theranos' Technology
They kept invoking trade secrets with everyone. You know, you couldn't see the machine, you couldn't really verify the claims, because they were afraid that their secret sauce would leak out and the incumbents in the lab industry, namely Quest and LabCorp, would get their hands on this technology and put Theranos out of business. And unfortunately, a lot of people believed this, you know, running the gamut from board members to journalists to these billionaire investors.

On the Harms Done by Theranos
That's the most egregious part of this scandal, is that she and her boyfriend, Sunny Balwani, who was the number two of the company, knew as they were rolling out the blood testing services in Walgreens stores in California and Arizona that the blood tests were faulty, and yet they still went ahead with the rollout. And there were … I came across personally in my reporting more than a dozen patients who had health scares because they received bad results from Theranos.

On How Holmes Fooled So Many People
I think … she capitalized on this yearning there was, in Silicon Valley and beyond, to see a woman break through in this man's world in Silicon Valley. If you look back over the past 30 years, all these tech founders that have gone on to be billionaires and icons were all men. Elizabeth Holmes was going to be that first [female] tech founder who became a billionaire.

8

The Media's Role in Promoting Tech Companies
Pew Research Center

The Pew Research Center is a nonpartisan think tank based in Washington, DC.

The Pew Research Center's study of media coverage of the tech industry, turned in at the end of the first decade of the new century, offers trenchant insights into the role media plays in establishing brands. Vital to the establishment of household names like Apple, Google, and Facebook was the work of their furtive public relations teams, tasked with delivering glowing coverage of their products in mainstream media outlets. But press coverage could also be finicky, as can be seen in the decade that followed. Many of the same media outlets that lauded companies like Facebook and Twitter as vital democratic platforms this time would later blame them for the spread of misinformation in the years following the 2016 presidential election.

In the battle among the tech titans, Apple Inc. won the title in the last year for press appeal. The 34-year-old company attracted more coverage from the mainstream press than any other technology company—and the bulk of it was positive. Its popular devices and orchestrated PR strategy helped it even outpace Google Inc.

"Apple Outpaces Google in Media Attention—Both Get Positive Play," Pew Research Center, September 27, 2010.

From June 2009 through June 2010, 15% percent of the technology stories focused primarily on Apple, versus 11% about Google.

The two social media platforms, Twitter and Facebook, came next (7% and 5%). Twitter's coverage during this time period largely centered around its communication role during the Iranian protests in the summer of 2009. Attention to Facebook was largely focused on the service itself and its interaction with its users.

Microsoft, on the other hand, received little press at all. After being arguably the most important technology company, even as recently as five years ago, run by the richest man in the world and the world's most powerful monopoly, Microsoft has, at least for now, fallen off the mainstream media's radar. It received just one-fifth the coverage of Apple, less than a third the coverage of Google and less than half the attention of Twitter. The one area of attention came in the search agreement with Yahoo in which Yahoo searches are now run on the Bing search engine. As this July 29, 2009, *Wall Street Journal* article explains, "Under the deal, Yahoo will make Microsoft's Bing search engine the search provider on its Web sites, licensing its own search technology to Microsoft to integrate if it chooses."

But the media paid little attention to any other technology players. No other company, including technology giants such as Amazon, Best Buy or Yahoo, registered more than 1%. And in covering these companies, the mainstream press focused heavily on the positive.

The media's take on Apple from June 2009 through June 2010 would make Steve Jobs proud. More than 40% of the stories about Apple suggested that its products are innovative and superior in quality. [Note: stories may carry more than one thread so the totals may not add up to 100.]

In this June 23, 2010, USAToday.com review of the iPhone 4, the author asserts, "The new iPhone….demonstrates once again why Apple's handset is the one to beat, even as it faces fierce competition from phones based on Google's Android platform, among others."

Another quarter of stories, 27%, highlighted the company's loyal fan base. Often this had to do with announcements of new products, such as this June 7, 2010, USAToday.com article about the imminent announcement of the iPhone 4: "It doesn't matter that the iPhone is now in its third year and that what is likely to emerge is merely an update. Legions of tech geeks, Apple competitors and ordinary consumers will be hanging on Jobs' every word."

And what about problems like ineffective touch screen, poor connections or limited user freedoms? Hard to find in this media coverage—just 17% suggested the products are overhyped, and less than half that, 7%, portrayed the company as too controlling with its products.

In Google's case, positive themes governed the coverage as well, though not quite to the same extent as Apple. Half as much of Google's coverage as Apple's, (20% versus 42%), portrayed its products as innovative and superior. In this May 11, 2010, MSNBC Live clip CNET analyst Maggie Reardon says that "One key difference that techy geeks talk about is multitasking, something that you are able to do on an Android phone that you can't do on an iPhone."

But even more stories, 25%, emphasized Google's help in navigating the Web by making content more searchable and easier to find. However, the third most prominent thread about Google was a negative one.

The theme that gave Google the most trouble is one that often accompanies a fast-growing, dominant company within any industry. The idea that the company has too much information and too much power appeared in 19% of the stories about Google (the third most-mentioned thread overall). This idea appeared in a story on Fox News Live about a scandal where Google streetview cars were accidentally collecting personal information.

Google was largely off the hook in the media's eyes, however, when it came to accusations that the company steals others' content, including the news media's. This theme emerged in just 2% of the stories.

For the two most written about social media networks, Twitter and Facebook, fewer distinct themes have emerged at this point. The two competing ideas surrounding Twitter are that the network helps disseminate information and connect people and that communication there is often pointless and self-centered. In this coverage, especially centered on Twitter's role in Iran, the positive influence heavily dominated. More than two-thirds of stories (68%) highlighted its role as a disseminator of information, while just 4% focused on the pointless nature of posts.

Facebook received largely positive press as well, though it suffered some from controversies surrounding its privacy settings. Most stories, 36%, articulated the value of Facebook in fostering communication; another 17% extolled its related role in bringing people together. But more than a quarter discussed users' dissatisfaction with Facebook's privacy changes and Facebook's attempt to alleviate those concerns.

9

Celebrities Have the Power to Push for Privacy from the Media
Marcel Berlins

Marcel Berlins was a French lawyer who ran a legal column in the Guardian *until 2010.*

Sometimes we turn to media for stories about the perpetuation of great injustices, about the corruption at the hands of public servants, and for a richer understanding of the lives of others around the world. Other times, we're looking for photos of celebrities. In one of his legal columns for the Guardian, *Marcel Berlins looks at how those celebrities use the legal system to navigate the paparazzi industry that services these images. He narrows his lens onto a law passed in 1998 that promises British citizens a certain right to keep images of themselves out of the media ecosystem. Shortly after, actors Michael Douglas and Catherine Zeta-Jones availed themselves of that law after a tabloid called* Hello! *secretly took some photos of their wedding. (They had sold the photo rights to a rival publication.) In that round,* Hello! *was forced to pay the rival over $1 million. In the decades since, entire publications—most notably a blog called Gawker in the United States— have been forced out of business by these kinds of verdicts.*

So now we know. There is such a thing as a legal right to privacy. Our judges have said so. But the irony is that the case that

---

"Now You See Us, Now You Don't," Guardian News & Media Limited, January 8, 2001. Reprinted by permission.

spelled it out was not about some sensitive, shrinking celebrity anxious to avoid prying paparazzi lenses or intrusive tabloid inquiries. On the contrary, the people seeking to assert their right to privacy had deliberately courted massive publicity and had been paid a huge sum of money to allow themselves to be seen in the world's media.

The problem was that the publicity that Michael Douglas and Catherine Zeta-Jones received for their New York wedding in November wasn't exactly what they wanted. They asked the courts of England to rule that, even though they had sold off a part of their privacy for £1m, they were still entitled to the protection of the law. The judges, citing our new Human Rights Act, agreed.

The wedding of the year (until it was supplanted by Madonna's) was held at the Plaza Hotel under conditions of absurdly exaggerated security. The reason was not so much the possibility of gatecrashers as the far more horrifying threat of uninvited cameras. Douglas and Zeta-Jones had signed a contract giving *OK!* magazine exclusive rights to taking and publishing photos of the nuptials. Invited guests were sternly warned not to bring cameras; they were electronically frisked anyway. Everyone working at the wedding signed a draconian contract promising not to take snaps, on pain of unimaginable legal consequences if they disobeyed.

But some cameras did sneak in, including one whose portfolio of nine not very good photos found its way to arch-rival *Hello!* magazine, which, to *OK!*'s dismay, was to publish them three days before *OK!* went on sale.

And so to court. *OK!* raised several legal issues in its—ultimately unsuccessful—attempt to stop *Hello!* from publishing. But the point that raised the privacy issue came from the Douglases personally. They want to sue *Hello!* for damages for breach of privacy. But surely they had abandoned their right—or sold it—by allowing the ceremony and reception to be photographed, and the results published?

Not quite, said Lord Justice Sedley in the appeal court. They had insisted on a veto over what photos were to be used, "in order to maintain the kind of image which is professionally and personally important to them." By retaining that editorial control, they were in effect saying that any pictures other than those personally chosen by them invaded their privacy.

The appeal court decided that the newlyweds were likely to succeed in any claim for damages against *Hello!* for breach of privacy. Whether in fact they win their case and how much they will get if they do is for a future court to decide. What's important is that this was the first case in which an English court has specifically said that we now have a law of privacy to protect individuals. The second case may well come later today, with a decision on the claim of the two killers of James Bulger to be granted lifetime anonymity. The Human Rights Act gives them the right to be left alone, free from media prying, they say.

But there is another twist to the law. The right to privacy arises because Britain has incorporated the European Convention on Human Rights into our national laws. Article 8 says that "everyone has the right to respect for his private and family life." But a little way further is Article 10, which guarantees the freedom of expression and freedom of the press. When the media want to publish something—whether information or pictures—about someone's private life, the two are bound to clash.

The Human Rights Act exhorts the judges to have particular regard to freedom of expression when deciding which way to rule, and gives the media a public-interest defence against anyone trying to stop them from publishing. That still leaves the judges with a sensitive balancing act to perform, and it is by no means clear which way they will turn when faced with a free speech-versus-media intrusion dilemma.

Other countries in Europe which have had privacy laws for decades don't always provide clear-cut solutions. In France, celebrities—Catherine Deneuve, Isabelle Adjani and Brigitte Bardot among them—are used to going to court to complain that photographs have been taken of them without their consent, but the line between private and public occasions has often proved hard to draw.

Until recently, the French press has been particularly timid in revealing information about politicians, even where it would have been in the public interest. The late President Mitterrand's cancer, surely relevant to his capacity to carry out his duties, was kept from the nation virtually throughout his presidency, as was the existence of his daughter by a long-term lover—though that revelation might not have met the public interest test.

The French privacy laws have also had a chilling effect in an area that worries the British media—the investigation of wrongdoing and corruption. It is generally accepted that crooked businessmen and dodgy politicians are more easily able to escape scrutiny because of the deterrent effect of privacy laws.

In Germany, with its relatively recent experience of dictatorship, the right to free speech is treated with particular reverence. German judges are constantly having to balance it against individuals' claims that their privacy has been invaded. In one case, the court had to decide whether or not photos taken of Princess Caroline of Monaco in a restaurant were a breach of her privacy. What signals was she giving to the media? the court asked.

Put simply, if she and her companion chose a secluded table well inside the restaurant, not easily seen from the street, the message was: "Lay off, this is a private meal." If, however, they sat at a prominent table by the window, taking snaps of her would not infringe her privacy. The decision went in her favour because of where she decided to dine. Is this the kind of balancing act that our judges will have to perform each time a case comes before them alleging an invasion of privacy? Probably, yes.

When the Duchess of York sought advice on blocking publication in the English tabloids of pictures showing her cavorting topless and having her toes sucked by her "financial adviser," she was firmly told that there was no law of privacy that could help her. By contrast, in France, a magazine that published those pictures not only had to pay the duchess damages for infringing her privacy but was punished in the criminal courts with a fine. If a similar case were to come before an English court today, would she be able to stop such photos being published?

On one side of the argument, the pics were taken, without her knowledge or consent, when she was on a private holiday in France, staying in a private villa, by a paparazzo using a long-lens camera from an adjoining property. On the other hand, there was the importance of the freedom of the press, the fact that the duchess had previously milked the media for publicity when it suited her, and the legitimate public interest in knowing that a prominent royal had exposed her children, the Queen's grandchildren, to the sight of her poolside frolics.

Would she have won? Perhaps. Would Diana, Princess of Wales have succeeded in banning the photos of her working out in the gym if there had been a privacy law? In fact, Diana didn't know in advance of their publication, so she couldn't have stopped it. Such victims will now be able to sue for damages, but a lot will depend on how much they are awarded. If the judges start handing out large sums, it could have a big deterrent effect on the media.

The appeal court's decision in the Michael Douglas case gives a few—but only a few—pointers to the way judges will look at privacy cases in future. Basil Markesinis, professor of civil and common law at University College, London, an expert on the privacy laws of various European countries, praises Lord Justice Sedley's "bold" judgment. "German case law shows that a balancing act can work without resulting in a flood of claims or the suppression of free speech. It also shows how it can be done on the basis of logical criteria, rather than by relying on accidents of history and litigation, which is how English law in this area developed in the past."

But it is impossible to predict how effective the privacy law will be in shielding celebrities or other newsworthy people from media attention and exposure. It is boring, but necessary, to emphasise that each case will give rise to different factors to be weighed in the balance. We now have a privacy law. How it will work in practice is in the uncertain and unpredictable laps of the judges.

10

Analyzing How Media Covers a Debate
The Roosevelt Institute
The Roosevelt Institute is a New York–based think tank named after the 32nd president of the United States.

The liberal think tank's media study also looks at how media coverage converges around a topic. Here, it's the argument over raising the minimum wage in the United States, a recurrent talking point for the past decade. The subject generated at least 273 articles in 2014, all of which the Roosevelt Institute studied to create a singular image of the subject's shadow in the media's eye. Stretching across the wealth of writing on the issue, a common narrative emerges: a complex conversation about wealth and inequality is reduced to a simple binary, one that bears an uncanny resemblance to the central red and blue lines of contemporary American politics. Raising wages across the board will either help millions to make "ends meet" or it will cost them their job, the study finds. A vague empathic balm faces off against a message of fear and scarcity. As of this writing, the baseline minimum wage in the United State remains at $7.25 an hour.

The purpose of this baseline media analysis was to understand what narratives around minimum wage are being covered in the media, with a particular focus on coverage of the impact of minimum wage on the economy.

"Media Coverage of Raising Wages," The Roosevelt Institute. Reprinted by permission.

An analysis of 273 articles published in 2014, mostly from print media, on raising wages found that:

- The coverage was mostly positive, driven by proponents of raising wages, who were quoted twice as often as opponents.
- The two most dominant narratives were the helpful impact of raising wages on the ability of workers to support themselves and the economic harm that raising wages would do, mostly by increasing unemployment.
- The leading messengers for raising wages were:
  - Elected officials, who made both the "make ends meet" and economic benefit argument.
  - State and local advocacy groups, who largely made the "make ends meet" argument.
- The leading messengers opposed to raising wages, who almost entirely made the economic harm argument, were elected officials and business associations.

The findings emphasize the need for proponents of raising wages to integrate both the positive impact on workers' lives and the economic boost from raising wages into their messages, so that advocates are not constantly on the defensive with respect to the economic impact of raising wages.

Articles in Database

We analyzed 273 articles, from throughout 2014. Most were taken from a national compendium of coverage on raising wages, collected by the media firm Berlin-Rosen. In addition, we added clips collected by Citizen Action of New York and Wisconsin Jobs Now. We deleted articles from the trade press.

Outlets: Primarily Local Print

Three-quarters of the coverage in the database is by local media outlets, almost all newspapers (print and online), in addition to a few local TV and radio stations. This actually understates the amount of coverage on local campaigns, as the subject of many of the articles in national news services and blogs were of local and state minimum wage campaigns.

We analyzed articles from outlets in 34 states. The campaigns that generated the most coverage were in: Seattle, Los Angeles, Chicago, San Francisco and San Diego. In addition Wisconsin and New York were represented more heavily, as we used clips collected by organizations based there.

The database included:

- Local print: 70% (192)
- National news services: 6% (17)
- National TV—cable and broadcast: 6% (17)
- National print: 6% (16)
- Local TV: 5% (15)
- National blogs: 4% (10)
- National radio: 1% (4)
- Local radio: 1% (2)

Subjects: Primarily State and Local Minimum Wage Laws
More than half of the articles were about state and local measures to raise the minimum wage. A little less than one-third focused on raising the federal minimum wage. And one-out-of-six were either about organizing aimed at employers (primarily Fight for $15) or employers deciding to raise wages on their own.

Of the 37 articles that talked about a protest or rally, 20 were on the Fight for $15. Looked at another way, 44% of the coverage about the Fight for $15 included protests, while only 7% of coverage on legislation included a protest or rally.

Subjects of coverage:

- 58% focus state or local wage hike
- 30% federal
- 16% Fight for $15
- 14% talk about a rally or protest

Messengers

Supportive Messengers: Elected Officials and Organizations Supporting Raising Wages

Two-thirds (68%) of the articles quoted an elected official (or appointee) who supported raising wages. Mayors who were advocating raising the minimum wage in their city led the list, followed by governors and then President Obama.

Half (55%) of the articles either quoted or referenced the support of an organization. A total of 225 supportive organizations were mentioned. The most frequently named organizations were the wide variety of state and local groups and coalitions who support raising wages. National advocacy groups followed, with NELP dominant, mostly because of its release of data on the number of people impacted. Two think tanks were also quoted for releases of specific data: EPI largely on increasing minimum wage not having an impact on jobs; and CEPR on a report that states that had raised their minimum wage had stronger job growth.

One-fifth of the coverage quoted a low-wage worker. Only 10% quoted a businesses owner or association that supported raising wages.

Here is the complete breakdown of supportive messengers as a percentage of all articles:

- Elected officials: 67% (185)
- State/local advocacy group or coalition: 36% (99)
- A national advocacy group: 25% (57). NELP was referenced in 36 articles.
- Worker: 22% (60)
- Think tank: 12% (32)
- Union or worker organization: 10% (27)
- Business owner: 7% (20)
- Economic development or business association: 3% (8)

Opposition Messengers: Elected Officials and Business Trade Associations

About one-fourth (28%) of the articles quoted an elected official (or appointee) who opposed raising wages, mostly governors or US Senators.

One quarter (27%) of the articles either quoted or referenced the opposition of an organization. A total of 99 opposing organizations were mentioned, dominated by business associations, notably state branches of the National Restaurant Association. Individual business owners who opposed wage hikes were quoted in 14% of the articles.

Here is the complete breakdown of opposition messengers as a percentage of all articles:

- Elected officials: 28% (76)
- Local business associations: 21% (56)
- Business owners: 14% (39)
- National business associations: 8% (23)
- Think tanks: 4% (12)
- National or state advocacy: 1% (3)

Narrative Elements

We analyzed the articles: the overall tone; the number and prominence of quotes on either side and the narrative themes. We included a more extensive analysis of the arguments around economic impact.

Overall Tone: Highly Positive, Dominated by Supportive Quotes

As would be expected when supporters of raising wages are running campaigns, the coverage was heavily dominated by quotes in support of raising wages, which were more prominently displayed. There were 621 supportive quotes, an average of more than two (2.27) per article, compared with 281 opposition quotes, one per article on average. The first quote was supportive in two-thirds (68%) of the articles, compared with only 14% of articles in which the first quote was opposed to raising wages. Overall, the researchers characterized two-thirds (65%) of the articles to have an overall positive tone toward raising wages, compared with 25% neutral and only 10% negative.

Summary of tone:

- Supportive quotes: 621—2.2 per article on average
- Opposing quotes: 281—1 per article on average
- First quote positive: 68% of articles
- First quote negative: 14% of articles
- Overall tone:
    - Positive—65%
    - Neutral—25%
    - Negative—10%

Dominant Narratives: Making Ends Meet and Economic Impact

Half (52%) of the articles talked about the impact of raising wages on workers' ability to support themselves. In addition half (50%) had some discussion of the economic impact of raising wages. One-third (35%) reported on the number of people who would benefit from raising wages. Only 8% talked about the hard work of low wage workers. Summary of narratives:

- Ends meet—52%
- Economic impact—50%
    - Harm the economy—41%
    - Benefit the economy—20%
- Many workers impacted—35%
- Hard work—8%

Making Ends Meet

The argument that being paid low wages makes it difficult to support a worker was made in half of the articles. It was most frequently made by advocacy organizations and workers, although elected officials also made the argument frequently. Here are some examples:

> "It's entirely impossible to make a budget when living on a tipped income," said Melissa Fleck, an executive assistant for the activist organization Citizen Action, who spent 15 years working in restaurants until June 2013.
>
> "No one should have to choose whether they have to pay rent or pay for food," said Alberto Retana, executive vice president of Community Coalition of South Los Angeles.
>
> "It's a dollar an hour, that's something," she [Minneapolis hotel worker] said. "It just gives you a little bit more comfort. You just don't feel quite as on the edge. You feel like you can fill up your tank and go to the grocery store and not be quite as concerned."
>
> "A wage of $8.25 an hour is a poverty wage and just perpetuates the cycle of poverty." [Spokesperson for PLAN, Nevada advocacy group]
>
> "In the Lehigh Valley, more than 50,000 workers receive wages so low that they are forced to turn to supplemental nutrition assistance to feed their families, according to a recent report by anti-poverty organization Oxfam America." Oped by the Pennsylvania Council of Churches.
>
> "Everyone knows you cannot live on the minimum wage, and you cannot make ends meet on $290 a week." Dan Cantor, WFP.
>
> "Minnesotans who work full time should be able to earn enough money to lift their families out of poverty and achieve the American dream," Gov. Mark Dayton said in a statement.

Making Ends Meet vs. Economic Impact

A common narrative in the articles was that there are two competing narratives: the argument by proponents on "meeting ends meet" vs. the argument by opponents that raising wages will cost jobs. A good example of this dynamic is from an article in the *Arizona Republic* titled, " Does higher minimum wage stifle job growth?" The lead quote in the article is on the impact on workers. Having dismissed that, the article than turned to the economic question:

The issue is virtually one of morality for people like Tomas Robles Jr., the executive director of Living United for Change in Arizona, a Phoenix-based group that advocates for worker and immigrant rights. The group has joined the chorus calling for raising the federal minimum wage, a move that could affect 500,000 Arizona workers.

"We're not expecting a $60,000 annual salary out of this," Robles said. "But you should be able to provide for your basic necessities."

For Steve Chucri, president and CEO of the Arizona Restaurant Association, the wage issue means greater complexity in an industry often buffeted by heavy labor turnover and volatile food prices.

"It has eliminated jobs in restaurants," Chucri said of Arizona's minimum wage. "Some restaurants have done away with busboys entirely ... and now we're seeing price increases."

Economic Impact

Opponents of raising wages focus virtually entirely on claims of negative economic impact, particularly reducing jobs as well as raising prices, as typified in the quote above from The Arizona Restaurant Association.

Four-in-ten (41%) of the articles contained this argument, one made by all the various messengers listed above. Of the 113 articles with negative quotes, 86% were about economic harm, mostly job loss.

Most of the time, the argument about harming the economy did not have a counter-argument from supporters; only 30% of the articles that contained the claim of economic harm contained an assertion that raising wages would benefit the economy. On the other hand, 61% of the articles that included an assertion of economic benefit also included a claim of economic harm. This data is another indication of two competing narratives. Reporters, who almost always want to have quotes on both sides of an issue, are counting advocates argument on "making ends meet" as being opposed by harming the environment.

Quotes asserting economic harm were placed at the top or middle of the articles. The distribution of quotes asserting economic harm and benefit was similar, which makes sense since articles are almost always written to include competing claims next to each other. However, since so many more articles only included the claim of economic harm, the distribution of claims of economic benefit are somewhat lower down than those of economic harm:

Economic Harm:

- 30% at top
- 53% in middle
- 17% at bottom

Economic Benefit:

- 31% at top
- 45% in middle
- 24% at bottom

Supporters asserted that raising wages would have an economic benefit in 20% of the articles, half the number of the articles that a claim of economic harm was made.

The argument for economic benefit was uniformly around increasing consumer purchasing power:

> *The wage increases would pump an additional $22 billion into the economy, Cooper [EPI] says, noting that low-wage workers tend to spend most of their paychecks, while higher-wage employees save more.*
>
> *"Every dollar we increase the minimum wage results in 2,800 dollars in additional spending by that working family," said State Rep. Mark Nakashima [HI], citing a study on the subject. "As this money comes to them, it'll come right back into the economy, and will help spur the economy," added Governor Abercrombie.*
>
> *Jobs would be created by raising the minimum wage, not lost, because the added money flowing to workers would be high-velocity money, rapidly spent for food, rent, clothes, health and education. It would boost the entire economy. — Computer Services Consultant*

The new law will pump nearly $500 million into the local economy, "proving that a higher minimum wage fuels business and job growth," said Seattle Union President David Rolf.

Only occasionally were advocates quoted combining the end meets and economic benefit argument, as in:

Linda Meric, national executive director of 9to5, which helped spearhead the 2006 constitutional amendment, says that this small raise "puts a little more money in the pockets of Colorado's lowest-wage workers to spend on essentials that will help their families and our local economy. But it is still not enough."

An example of an elected official making both arguments is from former Maryland Governor Martin O'Malley:

"Nobody who works full time should have to raise their family in poverty," [Governor] O'Malley said, contending that raising the minimum wage also boosts the economy by giving workers more money to spend.

Elected officials were quoted most frequently making the case for economic benefit, in one-third (32%) of the articles with that claim. Most other advocates were rarely quoted making the economic benefit argument.

Messengers for economic benefit argument:

- Elected officials—36%
- Business—5 or 10%
- Local advocacy groups—8%
- Think tank—12%
- National advocacy—4%
- Academic—2%
- Asserted without reference to any one group or individual—26%

Conclusion

The goal of this review of 2014 press coverage of raising wages was to understand how the press is reporting the narratives made by advocates for raising wages, with a focus on coverage of the economic benefit of raising wages. The findings confirm that the central narrative thrust of the press coverage is that raising wages will help workers support their families but it may cost jobs.

These findings underscore the need for advocates to:

- More vigorously assert the economy boosting argument and do so in a way that ties to the "make the ends meet" argument, so that we are framing the debate around both arguments, rather than being defensive on the economy.
- Engage more business owners and business groups that support raising wages, as they are credible messengers on that issue, particularly as those are (along with elected officials) the leading spokespeople for the opposing economic argument.
- Work with elected officials to effectively make both the make ends meet and economy boosting argument, as they are the most frequently quoted supporters in press coverage.

11

A Global Fast Food Workers' Movement Is Bolstered by Media

Annelise Orleck

Annelise Orleck teaches history at Dartmouth College. One of her more recent books is Rethinking American Women's Activism, *which was published in 2014.*

Reading a labor historian's take on wage protests among McDonald's workers gives us a chance to take our own look at how an issue dissolves into the rich talking points that define traditional media coverage. There are intimate stories of hardship and clever slogans: Orleck writes that alienated employees have taken to twisting the company's "I'm Lovin' It" slogan into something that means exactly the opposite. An event, when it goes on long enough, generates its own media-driven momentum. It's no longer a news oddity but a way of life, a constant protest, a saturation point that generates an understanding in the marketplace that this is what a once-beloved brand now means. McDonald's, its workers say, are not lovin' it.

When it comes to their wages, McDonald's workers around the world are not "Loving It"—and they haven't been shy about expressing their discontent over the past four years.

"McDonald's and the Global Revolution of Fast Food Workers," by Annelise Orleck, The Conversation, September 5, 2016. https://theconversation.com/mcdonalds-and-the-global-revolution-of-fast-food-workers-64574. Licensed under CC BY-ND 4.0.

But this Labor Day, America's fast food workers can celebrate victories that have improved wages for some of them. And they can applaud a global labor movement of low-wage workers that they helped spark and continue to inspire.

In April, fast food workers led the most global strike in history. It took place in 300 cities, in more than 40 countries in every region of the globe. It was a day of action against what activists called "McJobs"—low-wage, precarious work. And it caught the attention of the world.

From Manhattan to Manila, from Tokyo to Toronto, fast food workers were joined in living wage protests by home health care workers, airport workers, retail workers and millions of others who are fully employed but do not earn enough to make ends meet.

Earlier in the year, 27-year-old Florida McDonald's worker Bleu Rainer drove from Tampa across the state to protest outside of the Republican debate at the University of Miami.

Chanting, "We work, we sweat. Put $15 in our checks," he says protesters succeeded in injecting the fight for a living wage into the feisty Republican debate, where billionaire candidate Donald Trump raised eyebrows by insisting that wages in the US are already too high.

When America's low-wage workers, a disproportionate number of whom are African-American, convened in Richmond, Virginia, this August, they vowed to continue fighting and tied their struggle to the larger battle to overcome American racism. They coined the new slogan: Black Work Matters.

As a labor historian, I became interested in the global fast food workers movement, which uses history, popular culture and social media to organize and make its case. Over the last year, I've talked to fast food workers in Tampa, New York, Los Angeles, Manila, Philippines, and Phnom Penh, Cambodia, among other places.

They are literally hungry for change and they are making change happen.

A Global Network

Like popular culture, the problems of today's work world are global. As the slogan goes, "McJobs Cost Us All." Vast, transnational low-wage employers like McDonald's and Wal-Mart drive wages down for everyone. With more than half of US workers earning less than US$30,000 a year in 2014, the poverty line for a family of five, it is not a surprise that the Fight for $15 movement has attracted workers of all kinds.

The movement is bigger than just the United States. In Manila, young Filipino activists in the RESPECT Fast Food Worker Alliance staged singing, dancing flash mobs in their nation's legislature to demand labor protections. And, in Moscow, fast food workers staged protests to highlight the fact that they were not teenagers working for "going out" money but adults trying to support families with inadequate wages.

Where did all this anger come from? In 2015, 52 percent of fast food workers in the US received public assistance to make ends meet. Many had to work two and three jobs. Some commuted to work from homeless shelters. Maia Montcrief from Long Beach, California, told me that she lives in a one-bedroom apartment with six people. She is one of the lucky ones.

Though fast food workers have protested at many global and localized chains, the main focus of their movement has been McDonald's. With 36,538 restaurants in 119 countries, McDonald's is the world's second-largest private employer. Only Wal-Mart employs more.

"Because McDonald's has employees everywhere," activist Bleu Rainer told me, "everything they do has a global impact that affects all workers."

Bleu's Story

Rainer is a 27-year-old McDonald's worker.

"I've worked in the fast food industry in North Carolina and Florida," Rainer told me, "and in eight years I've made no more than eight dollars and five cents an hour." He said that even when he was offered a promotion to manager, his salary did not increase.

"I have witnessed the torture of not having enough to afford rent, which led to me sleeping from house to house," Rainer says. "One time I even had to sleep at bus stops because I was homeless. I have had to rely on food stamps just to get a good meal and when those food stamps run out it's back to nothing at all. Sometimes I think to myself: I'm working so hard every day. So why am I still hungry? Why am I not making a living wage? Why can't I feed myself?"

Beginning in 2012, Rainer and a small group of New York City fast food workers kicked off a protest against poverty wages. It was a decidedly 21st-century movement. They used one-day flash strikes instead of long-term actions that hurt workers more than employers. They deployed social media to organize and publicize their actions. And they gleefully subverted expensive corporate slogans—especially the McDonald's jingle "I'm Lovin' It," the first worldwide ad campaign for the burger giant, which they paid Justin Timberlake $6 million to sing on TV.

"Poverty Wages: Not Lovin' It" became the slogan of a new movement, and signs with those words soon appeared in as many countries and as many languages as the original version.

When I first met Rainer in Tampa, he was helping to organize a broad coalition of low-wage workers: fast food workers, home health care attendants and adjunct college professors—none of whom made enough money to pay their bills. As we sat together at a table in a West Tampa Cuban diner, the professors made clear that they saw themselves paddling in the same boat as fast food workers and home health care aides. They earned around $8 an hour, worked on short-term contracts and had absolutely no job security. "They try to convince us we're better, we're the elect," said Cole Bellamy, who teaches 12 courses a year. "But that's the lie they tell us to keep us quiet."

"We are all fast food workers," said graduate student Keegan Shephard.

"Or maybe we are all professor adjuncts," said Rainer.

The Successes

Their campaign has been remarkably successful in a short period of time.

This March, the National Labor Relations Board ruled that the McDonald's corporation is a joint employer of those who work in franchise-owned restaurants, a huge victory for fast food activists. Last summer, New York state granted a $15 minimum wage to the state's 180,000 fast food workers. Seattle, San Francisco and Los Angeles also passed $15 living wage ordinances. This spring, the state of California, which has a population of nearly 40 million people, passed a phased-in statewide $15 wage. The wages of federal food workers have been raised. Wal-Mart has raised its minimum. McDonald's offered increases to those who work in restaurants owned outright by the corporation, which pressured franchise owners to do the same.

Four years ago, when the first fast food workers' strikes were held in New York and Chicago, the $15 minimum wage seemed a fantasy. Now it is a reality in many of the largest labor markets in the US, and it is fast food workers who launched the tidal wave.

Yet, with all this success, the life of an average fast food worker is still difficult, at best. One reason most fast food workers are so poor is because their wages are so low. But it is also because computers scheduling shifts change workers' hours at the drop of a hat, making it impossible for parents of young children to plan child care or to know for sure whether they will be able to pay their bills each month. Algorithms, I have learned through numerous interviews, maximize efficiency for the company and cut labor costs whenever possible. Workers believe they are used to intentionally keep workers' hours low enough that they are not covered under state and federal labor laws and can be seen as part-time or temporary workers.

One McDonald's worker I met in New York City in 2015, who depended on his full-time salary, showed me a paycheck for two weeks' work that totaled $109.

Contrary to public opinion, most fast food workers are not teenagers on their first job but adults supporting families. The average fast food worker is 29 years old. Over 25 percent are parents. Nearly one in three have college degrees—or are working their way through college.

This is not the first time that restaurant workers have organized. Restaurant unions have, in different eras, been strong in some big cities, especially New York and Las Vegas. But this is the first time that fast food workers have organized, and it is definitely the first time that they have organized in conjunction with a range of other low-wage workers and on a global scale.

Massimo Frattini, a former hotel worker from Milan who is one of the global coordinators for fast food workers' actions, told me that he was stunned by the worldwide response when the first global strike took place in 2014.

On that day, fast food workers in 230 cities, in 34 countries, on six continents, walked off the job to dramatize their need for a living wage, full-time work and union recognition. The scale of the strike surprised pretty much everyone: the workers, the organizers and definitely McDonald's.

Workers staged mock trials of a weeping Ronald McDonald for wage theft in the streets of Seoul. They shut down McDonald's in Brussels and in London's Trafalgar Square.

"We were not aware of how organized workers were in the fast food sector in the Philippines or Thailand or New Zealand," Frattini said. "But the truth is they knew that alone, they were helpless against these massive corporations. But maybe together they could raise the issue on the global stage. And they could provide better services and negotiate better agreements for their members."

Over the next year, workers from New York, Chicago, and 150 US cities met with workers from Denmark, Argentina, Thailand, South Korea, the Philippines and numerous other countries. The Service Employees International Union in the United States and Frattini's international union of food, hotel and farm workers, which represents 12 million workers in 120 countries, paid for these meetings.

Workers compared notes on wages and working conditions. Workers from McDonald's and Kentucky Fried Chicken from every continent on Earth began planning strategy for global living wage agreements.

One of the original organizers, Naquasia LeGrand, was just a 22-year-old kid from Brooklyn who was tired of working three jobs. She looked back during the summer of 2016 on what she had helped start in 2012. She said: "We triggered something epic that had never been done." Indeed they had: a global fast food workers' revolution.

12

Politicians Use "Fake News" to Discredit Media

Andrea Carson and Kate Farhall

Andrea Carson is a professor at La Trobe University and co-editor of Australian Politics in the Twenty-First Century: Old Institutions, New Challenges *(2018). Kate Farhall is a research fellow at RMIT University.*

Not every news story reports just the facts on the ground, and rumors and outright fiction have always been found in the daily news. Here, Andrea Carson and Kate Farhall chart the progress of a phenomenon called "fake news" in Australian media. The term "fake news" took off during the 2016 US presidential campaign with regard to the spreading of outright fake claims on social media websites like Twitter and Facebook. But eventually, it evolved to became a talking point among conservative politicians around the world seeking to dismiss critical news coverage. The essential difference between the two kinds of allegedly "fake news," they say, is what is getting dangerously lost.

During the 2019 election, a news story about the Labor Party supporting a "death tax"—which turned out to be fake—gained traction on social media.

"The Real News on 'Fake News': Politicians Use It to Discredit Media, and Journalists Need to Fight Back," by Andrea Carson and Kate Farhall, The Conversation, October 1, 2019. https://theconversation.com/the-real-news-on-fake-news-politicians-use-it-to-discredit-media-and-journalists-need-to-fight-back-123907. Licensed under CC BY-ND 4.0.

Now, Labor is urging a post-election committee to rule on whether digital platforms like Facebook are harming Australian democracy by allowing the spread of fake news.

While the joint standing committee on electoral matters (JSCEM) will not report until July next year, our latest research finds that politicians are key culprits turning the term "fake news" into a weapon.

Following the election of Donald Trump as president of the United States, we investigated if Australian politicians were using the terms "fake news," "alternative facts" and "post-truth," as popularised by Trump, to discredit opponents.

With colleagues Scott Wright, William Lukamto and Andrew Gibbons, we investigated if elite political use of this language had spread to Australia. For six months after Trump's victory, we searched media reports, Australian parliamentary proceedings (Hansard), and politicians' websites, press releases, Facebook and Twitter communications.

We discovered a US contagion effect. Australian politicians had "weaponised" fake news language to attack their opponents, much in the way that Trump had when he first accused a CNN reporter of being "fake news."

Significantly, these phrases were largely absent in Australian media and parliamentary archives before Trump's venture into politics.

Our key findings were:

- Conservative politicians are the most likely users of "fake news" language. This finding is consistent with international studies.
- Political users were either fringe politicians who use the term to attract more media coverage, or powerful politicians who exploit the language to discredit the media first, and political opponents second.
- The discourse of fake news peaks during parliamentary sitting times. However, often journalists introduce it at

"doorstops" and press conferences, allowing politicians a free kick to attack them.
- ABC journalists were the most likely targets of the offending label.
- Concerningly, when the media were accused of being fake news, they report it but seldom contest this negative framing of themselves, giving people no reason to doubt its usage.

Here is one example of how journalists introduce the term, only to have it used against them.

Journalist: Today, we have seen a press conference by President Trump where he has discussed at length this issue as fake news. Prime Minister Turnbull do you believe there is such a thing as fake news?

Prime minister: A very great politician, Winston Churchill, once said that politicians complaining about the newspapers, is like a sailor complaining about the sea—there's not much point. That is the media we live with.

This kind of sequence suggests journalists play a role in driving and reinforcing fake news discourse to the likely detriment of trust in media.

One Nation's Malcolm Roberts provides the most extreme example of the weaponisation of fake news discourse against mainstream media:

Turns out the ABC, in-between spewing fake news about our party, ruined ANZAC day for diggers....The ABC are a clear and present threat to democracy.

Roberts was not alone. Politicians from three conservative parties claimed the ABC produced fake news to satisfy so-called leftist agendas.

What we discovered is a dangerous trend: social media users copy the way in which their politicians turn "fake news" against media and spread it on the digital platforms.

Despite this, our findings, published in the *International Journal of Communication*, offer hope as well as lessons to protect Australian democracy from disinformation.

First, our study of politicians of the 45th Parliament in 2016 shows it was a small, but noisy minority that use fake news language. This suggests there is still time for our parliamentarians to reverse this negative communication behaviour and serve as public role models. Indeed, two Labor politicians, Bill Shorten and Stephen Jones, led by example in 2017 and rejected the framing of fake news language when asked about it by journalists.

Second, we argue the media's failure to refute fake news accusations has adverse consequences for public debate and trust in media. We recommend journalists rethink how they respond when politicians accuse them of being fake news or of spreading dis- and misinformation when its usage is untrue.

Third, academics such as Harvard's Claire Wardle argue that to address the broader problem of information disorders on the web, we all should shun the term "fake news." She says the phrase:

is being used globally by politicians to describe information that they don't like, and increasingly, that's working.

On the death tax fake news during the 2019 election, Carson's research for a forthcoming book chapter found the spread of this false information was initiated by right-wing fringe politicians and political groups, beginning with One Nation's Malcolm Roberts and Pauline Hanson.

One Nation misappropriated a real news story discussing inheritance tax from Channel Seven's Sunrise program, which it then used against Labor on social media. Among the key perpetrators to give attention to this false story were the Nationals' George Christensen and Matt Canavan. As with the findings in our study, social media users parroted this message, further spreading the false information.

While Labor is urging the JSCEM to admonish the digital platforms for allowing the false information about the "death tax" to spread, it might do well to reflect that the same digital platforms along with paid television ads enabled the campaigning success of its mischievous "Mediscare" campaign in 2016.

In a separate study, Carson, with colleagues Shaun Ratcliff and Aaron Martin, found this negative campaign, while not responsible for an electoral win, did reverse a slump in Labor's support to narrow its electoral defeat.

Perhaps the JSCEM should also consider the various ways in which our politicians employ "fake news" to the detriment of our democracy.

13

Americans Are Divided in Their Trust of the News Media

Jeffrey Gottfried, Galen Stocking, Elizabeth Grieco, Mason Walker, Maya Khuzam, and Amy Mitchell

Jeffrey Gottfried, Galen Stocking, Elizabeth Grieco, Mason Walker, Maya Khuzam, and Amy Mitchell are all researchers and analysts at the Pew Center.

A Pew Center report finds that Americans' relationship to media is largely influenced by their own political leanings. It's a fundamental fact of bias: stories that add credibility to a worldview are believed faster and more readily than those that challenge our ideas and beliefs about the world. In a larger sense, however, the narratives that underline those political sensibilities also shape how media is seen as an institution. Conservatives, the authors note, are far more likely to think that journalists aren't willing to act ethically, a suggestion that nods at the past half-century of anti-media messaging used by political figures on the right.

It is no secret that, in an information environment characterized by deep tensions between President Donald Trump and national news organizations, Americans are divided in their trust of the news media. A new Pew Research Center exploration of more than 50 different surveys conducted by the Center—combined with an analysis of well over 100 questions measuring possible factors that

"Trusting the News Media in the Trump Era," by Jeffrey Gottfried, Galen Stocking, Elizabeth Grieco, Mason Walker, Maya Khuzam, and Amy Mitchell, Pew Research Center, December 12, 2019.

could drive trust in the news media—confirms that in the Trump era nothing comes close to matching the impact of political party identification. On item after item, Republicans consistently express far greater skepticism of the news media and their motives than Democrats, according to this analysis that focuses on trust in the news media during 2018 and 2019.

Even more telling, the analysis reveals that divides emerge *within* party—particularly the Republican Party—based on how strongly people approve of Trump's performance as president. Trump has publicly and repeatedly criticized both news organizations and the journalists who work for them, criticisms that, according to this study, resonate with his most fervent supporters.

The link between the public's approval of Trump and views of the news media is clear in evaluations of journalists' ethics. About three-in-ten Republicans and Republican-leaning independents (31%) say journalists have very low ethical standards, roughly six times the 5% of Democrats and Democratic leaners who say this. Trump's strongest approvers, though, express even greater suspicion: 40% of Republicans who strongly approve of Trump's job performance say journalists' ethics are that low. That is true of far fewer Republicans who only somewhat approve of Trump or disapprove of him: 17% and 12%, respectively.[1]

Overall, this relationship between support for Trump and depressed trust in the news media persists over a range of attitudes. And, taken together, Republicans who are most approving of Trump and Democrats who are least approving of him stand far apart from each other.

The extent to which a person is engaged with national politics and the news surrounding it also plays into their evaluation of the news media. Highly engaged partisans are even more polarized in their views than the two parties overall. For example, there is a 46 percentage point gap between all Democrats and Republicans (including those who lean to each party) in whether they have a great deal or fair amount of confidence that journalists will act in the best interests of the public. This jumps to a 75-point gap between the highly politically aware who associate with the two parties (91% of highly politically aware Democrats vs. 16% of highly aware Republicans).

No other factors in this study come close to these partisan dynamics in their relationship to Americans' views. There are a few that show some connection, however. One of these factors is trust in others more generally, or interpersonal trust: Americans who express greater trust in others tend to give the news media higher marks than those who are less trusting. Additionally, there are some interesting differences across demographic groups, such as those based on age, race and ethnicity, religion, and education. For example, black Americans often exhibit greater support of news organizations and journalists than Hispanic or white Americans. And older Americans are more loyal to their preferred news sources than younger Americans. Other concepts such as life cycle milestones and life satisfaction measures show limited, inconsistent or no relationship with evaluations of the news media.

The overall goal of this study was to integrate a wide range of concepts to develop a comprehensive understanding of the factors that link to the public's trust in the news media today. Researchers pulled together years of Pew Research Center surveys conducted on the American Trends Panel and examined responses from the panel members across these surveys. Using advanced statistical weighting and multivariate analyses, attitudes toward the news media—including direct measures of trust as well as closely related measures—were set alongside a wide range of other measures to examine what connects to trust in the news media.

Notes

1. There is a strong overlap between approval of the way Trump is handling his job as president and political party identification, but not a complete overlap. For instance, while most Republicans and Republican leaners strongly approve of Trump, the remaining Republicans are almost evenly split between somewhat approving of Trump or disapproving.

14

We Live in a Post-Truth Era
Ahmed Al Sheikh

Ahmed Al Sheikh is a former editor at Al Jazeera, a media network run by the royal family of Qatar, a small country in the Middle East.

Shortly after the 2016 presidential election in the United States, writes this Al Jazeera editor, it became clear that we were living in a post-truth era. It was not only Trump's election, but also Brexit, the rise of authoritarianism in democratic countries, and an increasing willingness to ignore concerns beyond one's borders. Western nations have abandoned ideals of liberalism, objectivity, integrity, human solidarity, and globalization. We now live in a world where people confine themselves to media bubbles, consuming only what we agree with and forgoing the collective whole of the outside world. But the same mechanisms that generated this post-truth moment can also save it, Al Sheikh argues.

In the social media era, everybody publishes whatever they want. Fake news websites are widely common, publishing lies and fabricated news. Far-right politicians in the post-truth era appeal to emotions and impose personal views; they hide the truth and convince people of what is untrue.

Where do mainstream media organisations stand in the post-truth era? How do they maintain people's trust, identity, credibility and originality?

"The Media in the Post-Truth Era," by Ahmed Al Sheikh, Al Jazeera Media Network, December 11, 2016. Reprinted by permission.

The British Oxford Dictionary made "post-truth" word of the year. It defines it as: "relating to or denoting circumstances in which objective facts are less influential in shaping public opinion than appeals to emotion and personal belief."

It is the post-truth era, when the West goes backwards and gives up the values of liberalism, objectivity, integrity, human solidarity and globalisation, which had been praised by many of its intellectuals. Francis Fukuyama, being one of them, once said (though later retracted his stance) that history ended here at the borders of political and cultural liberalism.

It is the post-truth era, when the West resorts to populism, which ushered in the likes of Donald Trump and will probably pave the way for rightist Francois Fillon, to win the elections in France, or perhaps even his rival the far-right leader Marine Le Pen.

It is the post-truth era, when Britain exits the European Union because it rejects the policy of open borders between member countries and only wants to benefit from the EU, but refuses to pay back.

It is the post-truth era, when Vladimir Putin slams the truth and oppresses every single opposing voice in Russia, supports the likes of Trump and Le Pen, and anyone else who calls for isolationism and chants the slogans "Russia First, France first, America first."

But how did we get here, to the post-truth era? And how can we get out?

A Far-Right and Social Media Symbiosis

We, journalists, have been happily using social media platforms since they appeared. We still stress their important role in spreading information. However, what we have witnessed during Trump's campaign, and those of far-right candidates on the other side of the Atlantic, is how social media has been exploited to disseminate untruths. It is like the old Arab proverb: The magic turned on the magician.

Social media was the most effective tool used by Trump and his right-wing Anglo-Saxon camp of people who could not accept a black president in the White House and who were worried that immigrants would replace them, despite themselves being descendants of settlers and immigrants. They used it to promote their electoral programme and encourage anti-liberal sentiments.

At the same time, Hillary Clinton's campaign was not as effective in mobilising voters on those platforms, appealing to their emotions or encouraging their populist instincts.

Trump's camp did not seek objectivity and integrity in their campaign, but their social media posts were immediately received by white voters as indisputable facts.

This is the problem with social media tools. They offer a quick way to convey one-sided information or opinion, without the option or capability to verify the authenticity of this information or to present the opposite opinion for the sake of balance.

By contrast, traditional media are platforms that pursue the presentation of opposing opinions and fully detailed objective information.

It is no surprise, therefore, that the far-right has found social media much more useful and conducive to their message than traditional media.

Peddling False Information

Another negative effect of the overuse of social media platforms to convey information and opinions is the bubble phenomenon, where users with matching political views exchange one-sided information and opinions that suit their own convictions, reinforcing them even further, even if those were based on false information.

Social media also distances people, because it limits communication to mobile phones. It deprives people of human contact and the accompanying intimacy and exchange of opinions, which could lead to changing a wrong impression or correcting an inaccurate belief.

Besides, tens of thousands of "fake news" websites have emerged, offering false information to an audience that is used to traditional media doing the fact-checking for it and that believes anything that appears on a presentable webpage.

With these websites and social media tools multiplying, it seems that we have become helpless and unable to stop the flow of false information or one-sided opinions.

This is the post-truth era! It is when lies replace the truth, emotions replace honesty, personal analysis replaces verified information and one opinion replaces multiple opinions.

This is the post-truth era, when extremists use social media as alternative communication channels to the mainstream media organisations (which used to ignore them) to promote their extremism.

Now, these same mainstream media organisations are considered an enemy and are being attacked constantly.

In days after Trump won the presidential elections, he would often go on social media and accuse media organisations of provoking protests against him.

He behaved like the leaders of what the West calls "the third world," many of whom have blamed Western media for their failure.

Using Social Media to Spread Truth

So, facing this juggernaut of misinformation, what do mainstream media organisations do? Mainstream media must use social media tools intensively in order to defend the truth, present the correct information and balance opinions.

Arab mainstream media is the most in need of this in the post-truth era, as the wave of racism and Islamophobia is strengthening representations of our culture and values as backwards and reactionary.

It is important to do an introspection and see what we are currently presenting to the young generations and how it does not properly challenge these hateful discourses. Most online media programming follows the idea that our youth want something fun and quick.

But, if we follow this logic in the content we produce, we will just encourage the shallowness of the youth's knowledge.

Who says our youth would not watch detailed and serious productions, if they were well-made, visually appealing and quick? Such production is not difficult to make.

Besides, our causes and torn realities deserve to be continuously presented to our youth, so that they learn from what happened in the past to prepare for the future.

For example, we need to remember and remind youth of what Britain's Mark Sykes, France's Francois Georges-Picot and Russia's Sergey Sazonov cooked up in 1916's agreement to partition the Ottoman Empire.

Arab mainstream media libraries are full of images and footage, and we can use the Sykes-Picot agreement material to make short videos and present them to our youth. This will urge them to think about what happened and what might happen with a "new Sykes-Picot" being planned in front of our own eyes in the Middle East.

Besides fun, light and quick productions, we can present to our youth the history of the Palestinian cause in short videos revealing the scope of the tragedy and the grave disappointment caused by friends and strangers alike.

Why don't we use these short videos to keep our youth constantly informed about the tragedies in Syria and Iraq and the miserable stories of refugees across the world?

Why don't we use those short videos to remind the youth of the nation's revolutionists who fought colonial powers, such as Abd al-Karim al-Khattabi, Ahmed Urabi, Abdelhamid Ben Badis, Ahmed Ben Bella, Hassan al-Banna, Gamal Abdel Nasser and others? Why don't we use them to reinforce in their hearts and souls the values of Arabism, religious tolerance and human solidarity?

All of this is possible if mainstream media organisations took it into consideration and adopted it as part of their visions.

In the post-truth era, mainstream media, and particularly TV channels, must formulate a clear vision based on their experience and expertise, away from amateur experimenting and imitating others. They must maintain the context of their core and original content, based on which they built their experience and people's trust, thus becoming their main asset.

In the post-truth era, mainstream media organisations must maintain their identity, in which they take pride in front of other people. They should never trade the elements of this identity with what does not suit them.

15

The Internet Changes Reporting, Too

Aleks Krotoski

Aleks Krotoski is a reporter and broadcaster who currently hosts a BBC Radio 4 program called The Digital Human.

The term "fake news" comes with an assumption of malice, but Aleks Krotoski takes a look at the impact that false reporting has when it mistakenly makes its way into mainstream news. TV networks have given credence to rumors spreading on Twitter. Newspaper stories have quoted shadowy online sources instead of questioning them. Krotoski's take on today's news channels isn't a fundamentally negative one, and his argument closes with how the internet's expanded reach has changed just what reporters and reporting can do.

For Peter Beaumont, this newspaper's foreign affairs editor, the revolution in Egypt revealed more than the power of the people in triumphing over repressive regimes; on a personal level, he discovered something new about his working practices.

Beaumont trained as a journalist in the days before the world wide web, but, like most of his profession, he has integrated new technologies into his news-gathering techniques as they've emerged. Covering the events in Cairo during the internet blackout in Egypt was like taking a step back in time.

"What Effect Has the Internet Had on Journalism?" by Aleks Krotoski, Guardian News & Media Limited, February 20, 2011. Reprinted by permission.

"We went back to what we used to do: write up the story on the computer, go to the business centre, print it out and dictate it over the phone," he says. "We didn't have to worry about what was on the internet; we just had to worry about what we were seeing. It was absolutely liberating."

The web's effect on news reporting is considered the most clear evidence that this is a revolutionary technology: news editors—and in some cases, the governments that they observe—are no longer the gatekeepers to information because costs of distribution have almost completely disappeared. If knowledge is power, the web is the greatest tool in the history of the world.

The process that happens before a story is published has also been transformed. The web has become the go-to point for the globe when it comes to getting information; it's the same for reporters. Online, they find a multiplicity of perspectives and a library of available knowledge that provides the context for stories. Increasingly, the stories are coming from the web.

Emily Bell, director of the Tow Centre for Digital Journalism at Columbia University and former editor of Guardian.co.uk, identifies coverage of the attacks on the World Trade Centre on 11 September 2001 as the incident that foreshadowed how events are covered today. "Linear TV just could not deliver," she says. "People used the web to connect to the experience by watching it in real time on TV and then posting on message boards and forums. They posted bits of information they knew themselves and aggregated it with links from elsewhere. For most, the delivery was crude, but the reporting, linking and sharing nature of news coverage emerged at that moment."

For reporters in Egypt, however, their greatest frustration was not that they were disconnected from the context provided by the network, but that they struggled to get their stories out. In fact, Beaumont found the silence a relief. "The way [Egypt] was reported didn't have all the ifs and buts coming from looking over your shoulder to try to figure out what the world is doing at the moment or who's saying what. You just had the news and the news was happening right in front of you."

More generally, technology has improved the processes of identifying stories that are newsworthy. Feeds from social networking services such as Facebook and Twitter provide a snapshot of events happening around the world from the viewpoint of first-hand witnesses, and blogs and citizen news sources offer analytical perspectives from the ground faster than print or television can provide. Paul Mason, economics editor on BBC2's *Newsnight*, uses these tools to get an angle on what's happening and what's important. "If you are following 10 key economists on Twitter and some very intelligent blogs," he says, "you can quickly get to where you need to be: the stomach-churning question, 'OK, what do I do to move this story on?'"

None the less, such tools are still only one element of the news-gathering process. This may mean that large organisations appear to break stories days after they've appeared on Twitter. "First-hand witnesses cannot see the big picture," says Yves Eudes, a reporter with French broadsheet *Le Monde*. "They're not trained to understand whether what they're seeing is relevant to the big picture or to see what really happens. They're trained to see what they want to see. If you only rely on Twitter or Facebook, you might end up howling with the wolves."

Indeed, in 2009, American TV networks found themselves in a very public mess when they reported the "Twitter line" on the story of a killing spree by Major Nidal Malik Hasan at Fort Hood US army base—that the killer had terrorist links. The details turned out to be false.

Eudes's caution does not mean he discounts the value of the tools the web offers its army of citizen journalists; *Le Monde* was one of the organisations, along with the *Guardian*, that worked with Julian Assange to publish the WikiLeaks cables last year. "Suddenly, we have all these new competitors that, if they're bold and well-organised, can change the course of news worldwide in a way that was completely unthinkable before the internet," he says. And loose organisations such as Global Voices, a network of international citizen journalists reporting on a global platform about local stories, offer windows on events around the world that are increasingly ignored by local papers.

Ultimately, however, Eudes believes the fundamentals of news-gathering have not been transformed by the web. "I need to know how to write or take a photo and I need to be good at analysis," he says. "Learning how to use tools is different from saying everyone is a reporter. Anyone can make bread, but it's lousy bread. You need to spend time like a true, professional baker to learn to make good bread."

Part of that learning process for newshounds, it seems, involves leaving the web and pounding the pavement for stories. For Beaumont, working from Tahrir Square without web access was a reminder of a purer form of journalism. "You forget that the internet, for all its advantages, is a distraction: you're always wondering whether what you're reading by others matches what you're witnessing yourself. If you don't have to worry about that, you can concentrate on pure observational reporting. Which," he says, "is a pleasure."

A pleasure that can only come from going offline.

16

Fake News Shakes Americans' Confidence
Michael Dimock

Michael Dimock is the president of Pew Research Center, where he has been since 2000.

Another Pew study reveals that media consumers, at large, conflate distinctions like fact and opinion when they consume news coverage, an observation that grants greater weight toward the perspectives of those who are doing the writing and reporting. The imprint of their beliefs and values become part of the story being told. As media becomes increasingly compartmentalized, more and more people adopt those worldviews as their own, no matter how niche they might be. An ostensibly nonpartisan institution like the Pew Center focuses on how these tendencies can be, nonetheless, thwarted so that rigorous and objective information can be piped in to compete with the opinion of political partisans.

A little over a year ago, Pew Research Center decided to intensify its research focus on the theme of trust, facts and democracy. The decision reflected a changing world: In the US and abroad, anxiety over misinformation has increased alongside political polarization and growing fragmentation of the media. Faith in expertise and institutions has declined, cynicism has risen, and citizens are becoming their own information curators. All of these trends are fundamentally changing the way people arrive at the

"An Update on Our Research into Trust, Facts and Democracy," by Michael Dimock, Pew Research Center, June 5, 2019.

kind of informed opinions that can drive effective governance and political compromise.

As part of this initiative, the Center has published more than 30 pieces of related research over the past 12 months. Two foundational efforts were our deep dive into Americans' views of the state of our democracy and our look at Americans' ability to distinguish between fact and opinion.

The first study found a glaring mismatch between the public's goals for American democracy and its views of whether these goals are being achieved. Out of 23 specific measures assessing democracy, the political systems and US elections—each widely regarded by the public as very important—there were only eight on which majorities said the country is doing even somewhat well. The second report explored the public's ability to process information in more detail by asking Americans to classify 10 statements they might see in the news as either factual or opinion. Just 26% of US adults correctly classified all five factual statements as factual—that is, something capable of being proved or disproved by objective evidence. Just 35% correctly identified all five opinion statements as opinion—that is, something reflecting the beliefs and values of the person who expressed it.

Today, we released a report that looks at misinformation in America. According to the study, many Americans say the creation and spread of made-up news and information is causing significant harm to the nation and needs to be stopped. Nearly seven-in-ten (68%) say made-up news and information greatly affects Americans' confidence in government institutions, and roughly half (54%) say it is having a major impact on Americans' confidence in each other. More Americans view made-up news as a very big problem for the country (50%) than say the same about terrorism (34%), illegal immigration (38%), racism (40%) and sexism (26%).

Of course, concerns about trust, facts and democracy are not confined to the United States. In an April report, we found broad frustration with the way democracy is working across the

27 nations we polled. In Europe, dissatisfaction with the way democracy is working is tied to factors including views about the European Union, opinions about whether immigrants are adopting national customs, attitudes toward populist parties and a sense that elected officials don't care about what ordinary people think.

Meanwhile, it's not just in advanced economies that there are concerns over the increasingly fast pace of digital communication and its effects on fact-based decision-making. A March study about mobile technology use in 11 emerging economies found that while people say mobile phones and social media are providing benefits, they are also concerned about these technologies' effects on children, as well as the technologies' role in purveying "fake news."

Over the next few months, we will release several reports examining more closely the state of trust among Americans. These reports will include findings about people's attitudes about specific institutions and groups, ranging from scientists and religious leaders to police, doctors and educators. They will also explore Americans' views about the reasons for declining trust—and how they think it might be restored.

The Center also will continue its exploration of the role that digital technology plays in the way people are navigating a more complicated information environment. Many Americans tell us that when making important decisions, they "do their own research" rather than trust expert advice. But most of that research still involves deciding which information to trust and what to ignore. And as a growing share of Americans depend on mobile devices for the vast majority of their digital engagement, the nature of that engagement continues to evolve.

Outside the digital realm, we will report on the changing nature of political and social discourse in US society. Building on our work on partisan polarization and antipathy, we'll explore what Americans deem acceptable speech and how that is shaped by political, social and moral factors. More broadly, we seek to understand how feelings of alienation from the rhetoric of our political leaders and anxiety over the pitfalls of talking about social and political issues in our personal lives might be changing the civic conversation at the center of our democracy.

And looking ahead to the 2020 election cycle, the Center will complement trends about partisanship, social identity, domestic and foreign policy priorities and overall confidence in our democratic system with a concentrated focus on understanding today's information environment and how it affects what people know and believe. Using the Center's American Trends Panel, our goal is to map Americans' relationship with news and information streams; track what they understand about the issues, events and candidate platforms; and study how demographic and political characteristics interact with these dynamics to shape preferences and attitudes over the course of the campaign.

All told, this body of work is meant to help explain how people in the US and around the world gather information and who they turn to as they try to make sense of it. We offer this data without recommendations for action. Rather, we hope this work serves the variety of innovative approaches being offered by citizens, civic organizations and policymakers who seek to channel the power of rigorous and objective information to inform decisions and strengthen democratic life.

17

The Center Loses Hold
Michael Griffin

Michael Griffin is a professor of history at Macalester College, with a focus on film and photography, media representation, media and culture/society, media institutions, journalism, and community media.

Media, it seems, was once so simple. There were newspapers that hired the best of the best. Trusted news programs delivered their insights through a comforting and respected voice of authority. Here, a media and cultures academic from a Minnesota liberal arts college details just how that system fragmented into the millions of little pieces that we now turn to in order to know what's happening in the world, from the digitized remains of the so-called legacy media brands to smart and savvy online influencers who can speak directly to the online niche that listens to them.

Many current concerns about the news can be traced back to long-term changes that began as early as the 1960s and accelerated in the 1980s, when media companies were bought by large conglomerates and chains, and increasing media concentration became a progressively larger problem.

In the middle of the 20th century, television network leadership believed that providing news was a public service. News wasn't expected to make money for national broadcasters. During that

"How News Has Changed," Macalester College, April 10, 2017. Reprinted by permission.

time CBS, for example, built up a high-quality news division, with distinguished journalists such as Edward R. Murrow opposing McCarthyism and Walter Cronkite, who became "the most trusted man in America," anchoring a highly respected nightly news broadcast watched by tens of millions. CBS also created foreign news bureaus around the world to inform the American public about international issues. It was referred to as the "Tiffany Network," alluding to the perceived high quality of CBS programming during the tenure of CEO William S. Paley. Network news was something that great numbers of Americans relied upon and could share; it gave them a common set of facts upon which they could have discussions and debates.

In 1986 CBS was bought by Loews Corp., then mainly a hotel and movie theater company headed by Larry Tisch. By the 1980s and 1990s these types of acquisitions were happening across the media industry, CBS and Tisch being just one example. Whenever a big entertainment company or conglomerate came in, the news divisions had to answer to shareholders and improve the bottom line. For the first time, there was an expectation that the news divisions had to make money, just like the entertainment divisions. And a major way to improve the profitability of the news was to cut costs. At CBS, cuts included the foreign bureaus, documentary division, and enormous numbers of people in the newsroom. This was an erosion of the concept and standards of quality news, and it happened precipitously in the 1980s and 1990s.

Then What Happened?

At the same time, market segmentation was increasing. As advertisers began to analyze large amounts of demographic data, they were able to target their products and advertising more precisely than ever before. Everything shifted to target marketing, and that means the national audience got sliced and diced. That happened first with magazines: the demise of the national general interest magazines—*Collier's, Life, Saturday Evening Post*—and the proliferation of thousands of little special interest magazines hyper-targeted to specific audiences.

Right after that came cable television. Instead of three channels (ABC, CBS, and NBC) dividing up a big, diversified national audience, cable TV came along and targeted narrow niche audiences. Instead of spending big money to reach a mass audience, advertisers could spend less money and reach the narrow demographics they were really seeking. The ad money moved away from the big networks, and the emphasis for news companies changed. News became just another commodity.

How Did Cable TV Change News?

Cable television's new 24-hour news cycle brought major changes. It meant newsrooms didn't have longer periods of time to prepare content, check it, edit it, vet it, and then present it to audiences. Reporters were pressured to go straight to air with current events and any new information that was presented to them. That began to result in rushed and incomplete reports, inaccuracy, distortion, and misleading material.

If you believe the polls, there's now a real lack of trust in the media among the public. Some polls show that more than half of Americans don't trust the media to tell them the truth. But this distrust isn't something that only began in the last election cycle. This trust has been eroding slowly and steadily for 30 or 40 years. And it is going to take a long time to build up again.

How Does Target Marketing Change What We See Online?

As a product of these targeted audiences, silos emerged. Silos create echo chambers, which characterized developments on television even before the web began to have a big impact. As the web opened access to the internet for a large number of people beginning in the late 1990s, it accelerated these echo chambers.

Everything about the way the web works—and the algorithms that track the patterns of your internet activity—reinforces the idea that there's a feedback loop that constantly redirects us toward what we're already interested in. It's a natural human quality to want your already-held opinions and perceptions about the world reinforced. The web specifically caters to that tendency. It creates patterns in which we only tend to look at—or even get access to—information that confirms our already-held positions.

And all of that matches up beautifully with the niche marketing and target marketing that's been going on for 50 years. What better information could advertisers get about your tendencies, tastes, interests, hobbies, and consumption patterns than what you're doing on the web? This tells advertisers almost perfectly what they want to know about you, and it solidifies the silos that are already in place. This has gotten worse as more and more people are on the web, more and more of the time. And it means that the traditional media continue to lose ad dollars. (Now we see that legislation has just passed the House of Representatives to allow internet service providers like Comcast and Verizon to sell records of our internet activities to businesses and advertisers.)

What Has That Meant for Newspapers?

In the early 2000s, newspapers weren't experiencing a significant readership dropoff yet, but they were starting to lose advertising money. Before the rise of the Web, if you lived in Minneapolis and you were looking for a used car, you'd go to the Star Tribune classifieds section, the paper's single biggest revenue source prior to the 2000s. When the web became more accessible, sites like Craigslist or Cars.com were more efficient resources. Who would still pore over the classifieds when you could just do a quick search online?

That was the first really serious blow to the traditional news media. When their ad and classified revenues dropped, the only recourse in their view at the time was to cut costs. By 2005–06, this was leading to massive layoffs in the newsroom. The newspapers became smaller, with fewer printed pages and less content. And then, not surprisingly, people weren't as interested in subscribing. A death spiral for newspapers began to develop.

Did Moving News Online Work?

When people tried to move newspapers to the web, they found out immediately that the print advertising mostly did not follow them online. As the newspapers were spiraling down, there simply was not the same number of reporters and editors doing serious journalism. There were blogs on the web, where lots of people were writing opinionated commentary, and aggregation sites that were recycling existing stories from other publications. But the amount of original reporting nationwide just began to diminish tremendously. Reliable quality news reporting, as opposed to content re-purposing and commentary, was no longer being supported in the same way by commercial, ad-supported news media institutions.

Because of this, there's no longer a model that most citizens in our country share for standards that news should meet. We're getting more and more of our news online, and more and more of that news—in Facebook feeds and web browsing—is suspect in terms of its status as news. When someone on Facebook sends me a story, the first thing I do is see where it's from. If it's from someplace I've never heard of, then red flags go up for me right away, and I check to see what that organization is. But most people do not have a working frame of reference for distinguishing different types of news sources.

How Is Online News Different from Traditional News?

There's not very much new original reporting on the web anymore, unless you go to the traditional news sites that are still run by traditional, respectable newspapers. We have fewer paid reporters than we did 15 years ago, and you're not going to get the same kind of coverage if you have vastly fewer people doing the work. But websites still have to fill up their spaces with content—so what do they fill it up with if they don't have verifiable original reporting? You see a decrease in actual news and an increase in opinion, commentary, and blogging, not to mention the vast quantities of frivolous entertainment-oriented content and click-bait.

In the online environment where information comes as a steady linear stream, where it's not divided up with a front page, an opinion page, and different specialized news sections (that prioritize news information according to prominence, urgency, civic importance, or local, national, and international orientation), it's all just mixed together. It's a relatively undifferentiated wash of stories and information. As a result, more and more young people don't have a clear notion of the distinction between something that's a news article and something that's just an opinion piece. It's all just "the next thing on the page" because they've grown up being online.

What Does That Mean for a News Consumer?

We don't just sit back and watch the evening news and believe Walter Cronkite when he says, "And that's the way it is," or pick up a daily newspaper feeling as though its editors will sort and summarize for us the important news we need to know about that day. We can't, or don't, do that anymore—and that's the challenge. Most people are so busy, with so many demands on them, that they don't have the time to carefully evaluate news sources. Most citizens today don't make carefully considered judgments about the sources they will routinely rely upon for sound information. They are more or less at the mercy of floods of content directed at them through algorithmic marketing mechanisms. Just look at the home page of any internet log-on page.

What About Paying for News Online?

The biggest crisis for journalism right now is this financial model for paying reporters to do serious reporting. Who's going to pay for the news? People are increasingly unwilling to pay subscription fees because they think they can go online and get everything for free. The news organizations that have managed to weather these changes are places like the *New York Times*, which took a stand and created a paywall to require subscriptions. At first, that seemed very risky. But it ended up working out okay for them, because they provide the kind of quality and in-depth news reporting that *New York Times* readers want and are willing to pay for. And now they've got a revenue stream of subscription money—and that means they don't depend entirely on advertising money.

What Can a News Consumer Do to Support Journalism?

Identify reliable, respectable sources—and then support those organizations as your primary sources of news and information. Subscribe or donate money if you can. If you don't have resources to donate, just go back to that source as a primary information source to support them with your readership, viewing, listening or online clicks. It doesn't mean those organizations are always correct and never biased—but they should conform to a set of stated standards. You know what their mission and motivations are, how they do their work, and you can hold them accountable.

That's what we have to look for as consumers. If you think the *Financial Times* of London is an honest, respectable source that isn't trying to fool you, read the *Financial Times* every day. If you find National Public Radio to be a good anchor that's doing its newswork in an honest way, then listen to NPR every day and send in a check for 20 bucks. Help support them, so they can keep doing what they're doing.

Can News Organizations Thrive in This Climate?

The *Washington Post*, another good information source, used to suffer from the same diminished ad revenues and bleak financial models that have plagued so many other newspapers. Any news organization that's owned by publicly owned companies (those that trade on Wall Street) is always trying to satisfying shareholders. They always have to think about short-term profits: how are we doing this quarter? At the *Washington Post*, Amazon owner Jeff

Bezos swooped in to buy the paper a couple of years ago and has stabilized its finances. Bezos basically said, "I think newspapers are really important, and I think the *Washington Post* is one of the jewels of our journalism system, so I'm going to buy it and run it as a private company that's no longer at the mercy of Wall Street. I'll keep the same editorial staff and the same reporters in place, and I'm going to let them do their job."

Since Bezos purchased them, we've seen the *Washington Post* become a much more aggressive news organization, because they're independently owned and they have a new kind of freedom. Note: they're not owned by Amazon—they're owned by Jeff Bezos, a private citizen and businessperson interested in supporting independent news sources. I'm all in favor of these kinds of purchases.

How Are News Organizations Responding to Recent Attacks on the Media?

Just as some have said that Donald Trump's election has inspired people to get out and be more active politically, the attacks on the press's credibility are awakening activism in support of good sources of news—and awakening a resolve in news organizations themselves to try to uphold the ideals on which they were founded. When the *Washington Post* puts on its masthead "Democracy Dies in Darkness," they're stiffening their resolve against the attacks and saying they're going to stand up for honest, accurate, and transparent journalism. The *New York Times*, with its traditional slogan, "All the News That's Fit to Print," has shown a similar resolve. The attacks could have an inadvertently positive impact over the long term. But it's up to people to support these organizations.

We're at a real turning point in media history. We're going to find out in the next 10 years whether viable, respectable, and honest news sources are going to survive. There's reason for hope in what's happening out there. But there are lots of uphill battles to be fought, and we're fighting against the trend of history. It's not going to be easy.

Organizations to Contact

The editors have compiled the following list of organizations concerned with the issues debated in this book. The descriptions are derived from materials provided by the organizations. All have publications or information available for interested readers. The list was compiled on the date of publication of the present volume; the information provided here may change. Be aware that many organizations take several weeks or longer to respond to inquiries, so allow as much time as possible.

Accuracy in Media
1717 K Street NW
Suite 900
Washington, DC 20006
(202) 364-4401
email: info@aim.org
website: info@aim.org
Accuracy in Media is a conservative group critical of mainstream media's liberal bias. One of the organization's most notable accomplishments was a documentary called *Television's Vietnam: The Real Story*, which argued that media coverage was responsible for America's loss in the Vietnam War. More recently, Accuracy in Media extensively criticized coverage of the COVID-19 pandemic in "mainstream media."

Columbia Journalism Review
801 Pulitzer Hall
2950 Broadway
New York, NY 10027
(212) 854-1881
email: editors@cjr.org
website: cjr.org

115

The *Columbia Journalism Review* is a journalism newspaper and website that has been published by the Columbia University Graduate School of Journalism since 1961. Currently run by the current editor in chief at Reuters, *CJR* regularly publishes researched stories on the state of reporting Today. Some of the best coverage *CJR* has run lately has been its behind-the-scenes retellings of how some of the major news stories of our time were researched and published.

Fairness & Accuracy in Reporting
124 W. 30th Street
Suite 201
New York, NY 10001
(212) 633-6700
email: fair@fair.org
website: fair.org

FAIR calls itself "the national media watch group." In addition to its work as a nonprofit, the group puts out a newspaper called *Extra!* and a radio show called *CounterSpin*, both of which also focus on the larger media stories that underline everyday news coverage. The organization, considered somewhat left-leaning, sees itself as a conduit between the activists who want to change the world and the reporters who are writing about it.

Journalism Education Association
105 Kedzie Hall
828 Mid-Campus Drive, South
Manhattan, KS 66506-1505
(866) 532-5532
email: staff@jea.org
website: jea.org

The Journalism Education Association is a nonprofit organization for teachers of journalism. It publishes the quarterly magazine *Communication: Journalism Education Today* and provides a public guideline of standards for journalism educators. The organization also trains journalism education mentors who have worked with journalism teachers around the world.

Media Freedom and Information Access Clinic at Yale Law School
Yale Law School
127 Wall Street
New Haven, CT
(203) 432-4992
email: publicaffairs.law@yale.edu.
website: law.yale.edu/mfia

The Media Freedom and Information Access Clinic is a law student clinic dedicated to "increasing government transparency, defending the essential work of news gatherers, and protecting freedom of expression." The group provides pro bono representation to news organizations, freelance journalists, academics, and activists. The group has also litigated FOIA cases that have compelled the release of information about the negotiation of the Trans-Pacific Partnership and the rules for closing the military commissions at Guantanamo.

Media Matters for America
PO Box 52155
Washington, DC 20091
(202) 772-8195
email: action@mediamatters.org
website: mediamatters.org

Media Matters for America is the project of Democratic Party operative David Brock, a formerly conservative newspaper columnist who started the group with the assistance of the Center for American Progress, a liberal think tank. Much of the group's work focuses on identifying right wing bias in news media, which it labels "conservative misinformation."

Media Research Center
1900 Campus Commons Drive
Suite 600
Reston, VA 20191
(571) 267-3500
website: mrc.org

Calling itself "America's premier media watchdog," the Media Research Center labels national news media the "the propaganda arm of the Left." Fittingly, it represents the conservative end of groups like FAIR and Media Matters. Among the issues that the group has been involved in is criticizing coverage of climate change.

National Freedom of Information Coalition
University of Florida, College of Journalism
and Communications
3208 Weimer Hall
Gainesville, FL 32611-8400
(352) 294-7082
email: nfoic@nfoic.org
website: nfoic.org

The National Freedom of Information Coalition has 45 state affiliates that task themselves with making sure state and local governments, as well as public institutions, have laws, policies, and procedures to ensure the public's access to their records and proceedings. The coalition is dominated by journalists and media lawyers, but their programs and work aim to help all citizens who seek public information. On its website, you can find sample FOIA requests and a tutorial on how the process of requesting information from government bodies works.

National Scholastic Press Association

2829 University Avenue SE
Suite 720
Minneapolis, MN 55414
(612) 200-9254
email: info@studentpress.org
website: studentpress.org

This national organization is aimed at supporting high school and college-based publications. The organization regularly hosts conventions celebrating high school newspapers around the country. Its annual awards, also aimed at stories published in high school newspapers, have been compared to the Pulitzer for high school journalists.

Pew Research Center

1615 L Street NW
Suite 800
Washington, DC 20036
(202) 419-4300
email: info@pewresearch.org
website: www.pewresearch.org

The Pew Research Center is a project started by Pew Charitable Trusts, a fund begun by the heirs of the Sunoco oil fortune. The center acts as a nonpartisan research center and is mostly well-known for its widely cited public opinion polling. It identifies as a nonpartisan "fact tank," and it regularly provides freely accessible analysis of its polling data.

Shorenstein Center on Media, Politics and Public Policy

John F. Kennedy School of Government
Harvard University
79 JFK Street
Cambridge, MA 02138
(617) 495-8269
email: shorenstein_center@hks.harvard.edu
website: shorensteincenter.org

The Shorenstein Center is a Harvard University journalism research center named after Joan Shorenstein, a journalist for the *Washington Post* who later produced *The CBS Evening News with Dan Rather*. It was originally funded by Shorenstein's father, a San Francisco real estate magnate. More recently, the journalism research center became the home of First Draft News, a non-profit founded by Google News Lab that works to fight mis- and disinformation online.

Bibliography

Books

W. Joseph Campbell. *Getting It Wrong: Ten of the Greatest Misreported Stories in American Journalism*. Berkeley, CA: University of California Press, 2010.

David Cromwell. *Why Are We the Good Guys? Reclaiming Your Mind from the Delusions of Propaganda*. Alresford, United Kingdom: Zero Books, 2012.

Drew Curtis. *It's Not News, It's Fark: How Mass Media Tries to Pass Off Crap as News*. New York, NY: Avery, 2008.

Nick Davies. *Hack Attack: How the Truth Caught Up with Rupert Murdoch*. New York, NY: Farrar, Straus and Giroux, 2014.

Kate Eichhorn. *The End of Forgetting: Growing Up with Social Media*. Cambridge, MA: Harvard University Press, 2019.

Andrew Fox. *Global Perspectives on Media Events in Contemporary Society*. Hershey, PA: Information Science Reference, 2016.

Ryan Holiday. *Trust Me, I'm Lying: Confessions of a Media Manipulator*. New York, NY: Portfolio, 2013.

Harold Holzer. *Lincoln and the Power of the Press: The War for Public Opinion*. New York, NY: Simon & Schuster, 2015.

Jamie Kilstein and Allison Kilkenny. *Newsfail: Climate Change, Feminism, Gun Control, and Other Fun Stuff We Talk About Because Nobody Else Will*. New York, NY: Simon & Schuster, 2014.

Charles Lewis. *935 Lies: The Future of Truth and the Decline of America's Moral Integrity*. New York, NY: PublicAffairs, 2014.

Robin Mansell. *Imagining the Internet: Communication, Innovation, and Governance*. Oxford, United Kingdom: Oxford University Press, 2012.

Debra L. Merskin. *The Sage International Encyclopedia of Mass Media and Society.* Thousand Oaks, CA: Sage, 2020.

Michael O'Shaughnessy, Jane Stadler, and Sarah Casey. *Media & Society.* Melbourne, Australia: Oxford University Press, 2016.

Eli Pariser. *The Filter Bubble: What the Internet Is Hiding from You*. New York, NY: Penguin Random House, 2011.

Elizabeth M. Perse and Jennifer Lambe. *Media Effects and Society*. New York, NY: Routledge, 2017.

Deana A. Rohlinger. *New Media and Society*. New York, NY: NYU Press, 2019.

Paul Starr. *The Creation of the Media: Political Origins of Modern Communications*. New York, NY: Basic Books, 2005.

Matt Taibbi. *Hate Inc.: Why Today's Media Makes Us Despise One Another.* New York, NY: OR Books, 2009.

Kevin M. Wagner and Jason Gainous. *Tweeting to Power: The Social Media Revolution in American Politics*. Oxford, United Kingdom: Oxford University Press, 2013.

Kevin Young. *Bunk: The Rise of Hoaxes, Humbug, Plagiarists, Phonies, Post-Facts, and Fake News*. Minneapolis, MN: Graywolf Press, 2017.

Periodicals and Internet Sources

Charlotte Alter, "How Conspiracy Theories Are Shaping the 2020 Election—and Shaking the Foundation of American Democracy," *Time*, September 10, 2020. https://time.com/5887437/conspiracy-theories-2020-election

Bibliography

Jay David Bolter, "Social Media Are Ruining Political Discourse," *Atlantic*, October 19, 2019. theatlantic.com/technology/archive/2019/05/why-social-media-ruining-political-discourse/589108

Timothy Burke, "How America's Largest Local TV Owner Turned Its News Anchors into Soldiers in Trump's War on the Media," Deadspin, March 31, 2018. https://theconcourse.deadspin.com/how-americas-largest-local-tv-owner-turned-its-news-anc-1824233490

Adrian Chen, "The Fake-News Fallacy," *New Yorker*, July 28, 2017. newyorker.com/magazine/2017/09/04/the-fake-news-fallacy

William Davies, "Why Can't We Agree on What's True Anymore?" *Guardian*, September 19, 2019. https://www.theguardian.com/media/2019/sep/19/why-cant-we-agree-on-whats-true-anymore

Economist, "Britons Are Increasingly Avoiding the News," August 20, 2020. https://www.economist.com/britain/2020/08/20/britons-are-increasingly-avoiding-the-news

Elizabeth Grieco, "U.S. Newspapers Have Shed Half of Their Newsroom Employees Since 2008," Pew Research Center, April 20, 2020. https://www.pewresearch.org/fact-tank/2020/04/20/u-s-newsroom-employment-has-dropped-by-a-quarter-since-2008

Jonathan Haidt and Tobias Rose-Stockwell, "The Dark Psychology of Social Networks," *Atlantic*, December 2019. https://www.theatlantic.com/magazine/archive/2019/12/social-media-democracy/600763/

Mark Jurkowitz, Amy Mitchell, Elisa Shearer, and Mason Walker, "U.S. Media Polarization and the 2020 Election: A Nation Divided," Pew Research Center, January 24, 2020.

https://www.journalism.org/2020/01/24/u-s-media-polarization-and-the-2020-election-a-nation-divided/

Cecilia Kang, "F.C.C. Opens Door to More Consolidation in TV Business," *New York Times*, November 16, 2017. https://www.nytimes.com/2017/11/16/business/media/fcc-local-tv.html

John Keane, "Post-Truth Politics and Why the Antidote Isn't Simply 'Fact-Checking' and Truth," The Conversation, March 22, 2018. https://theconversation.com/post-truth-politics-and-why-the-antidote-isnt-simply-fact-checking-and-truth-87364

David Leonhardt, "The Six Forms of Media Bias," *New York Times*, January 31, 2019. nytimes.com/2019/01/31/opinion/media-bias-howard-schultz.html

Stephen Marche, "How We Solved Fake News the First Time," *New Yorker*, April 23, 2018. https://www.newyorker.com/culture/cultural-comment/how-we-solved-fake-news-the-first-time

Jane Martinson, "Media Should Reflect All Society, Not Just a Typically Male Ruling Class," *Guardian*, September 17, 2017. https://www.theguardian.com/media/media-blog/2017/sep/17/the-media-should-reflect-the-whole-of-society-not-just-one-ruling-class-jane-martinson

Ariana Pekary, "CNN Public Editor: The Only Question in News Is 'Will It Rate?'" *Columbia Journalism Review*, September 2, 2020. https://www.cjr.org/public_editor/cnn-public-editor-the-only-question-in-news-is-will-it-rate.php

Eli Saslow, "'Nothing on This Page Is Real': How Lies Become Truth in Online America," *Washington Post*, November 11, 2018. https://www.washingtonpost.com/national/nothing-on-this-page-is-real-how-lies-become-truth-in-online-america/2018/11/17/edd44cc8-e85a-11e8-bbdb-72fdbf9d4fed_story.html

Ben Smith, "Journalists Aren't the Enemy of the People. But We're Not Your Friends," *New York Times*, September 6, 2020. https://www.nytimes.com/2020/09/06/business/media/trump-election-journalists.html

James B. Stewart, "When Media Mergers Limit More Than Competition," *New York Times*, July 25, 2014. https://www.nytimes.com/2014/07/26/business/a-21st-century-fox-time-warner-merger-would-narrow-already-dwindling-competition.html

Mike Wendling, "The (Almost) Complete History of 'Fake News.'" BBC Trending, January 22, 2018. bbc.com/news/blogs-trending-42724320

Index

A
advertising/advertising revenue, 11–17, 22, 44, 46, 47, 48, 49, 50, 51, 52, 108–109, 110, 111, 113
Akre, Jane, 14
Alter, Charlotte, 8
Anderson, Ross, 27

B
Bagdikian, Ben, 14, 15
Beaumont, Peter, 99–101, 102
Bell, Emily, 100
Bergman, Lowell, 12, 13–14
Berlins, Marcel, 62–66

C
cable tv, effect on news, 109
Carreyrou, John, 55, 56
Carson, Andrea, 19–23, 85–89
Cheema, Umar, 20
civic/public journalism, 46
Clark, Adam, 28
communitarianism, 11, 15, 17
Cronkite, Walter, 15, 108, 112

D
Demorest, Julie A., 11–18
Dewey, John, 11, 16, 17
Dimock, Michael, 103–106
Douglas, Michael, 62, 63, 66

E
Ehrlich, Matthew, 14–15
Elliott, Deni, 16, 17
Eudes, Yves, 101–102

F
fake news, use of to discredit media, 85–89
Farhall, Kate, 85–89
fast-food workers' movement, 78–84
Federal Communications Commission (FCC), 12, 13, 14, 41, 49, 51
Fleming, Jeremy, 26, 27
Frattini, Massimo, 83–84
Freedom Act, 27

G
Global Investigative Journalism Network (GIJN), and Nepal conference, 20–22
Gottfried, Jeffrey, 90–92
Grieco, Elizabeth, 90–92
Griffin, Michael, 107–114
Guensburg, Carol, 12

H
Hern, Alex, 24–29
Holmes, Elizabeth, 55–57

Index

Hulteng, John L., 17
Human Rights Act (UK), 63, 64
Huppert, Julian, 27

I

Idsvoog, Karl, 12
Investigatory Powers Act (UK), 27

K

Khuzam, Maya, 90–92
Kirtley, Jane, 12–13
Krotoski, Aleks, 99–102

L

Ledgett, Richard, 26
LeGrand, Naquasia, 84

M

MacAskill, Ewen, 24–29
Mason, Paul, 101
Matsa, Katerina Eva, 30–34
McChesney, Robert W., 43–54
McDonald's, 78–84
media bubbles, 93, 95
media literacy, 46
media reform, 43–54
minimum wage, media's coverage of, 67–77
Mitchell, Amy, 30–34, 90–92

N

news editors, responsibilities/role of, 11–17
news media, Americans' trust of, 7–8, 9, 90–92, 103–106
newspapers, effect of online news on, 110–114

O

Omand, Sir David, 27
Orleck, Annelise, 78–84

P

Panama Papers, 20
Pew Research Center, 30–34, 58–61, 103–106
Pew Research Center, and survey on media/media bias, 30–34
Pew Research Center, and update on misinformation and trust of media in America, 103–106
polls/elections, and media influence, 35–42
"post-truth," definition of, 94
post-truth era, the media and, 93–98
privacy laws and celebrities, 62–66
Project Censored, 13
public broadcasting, 47–49, 50, 54

R

Rainer, Bleu, 79, 80–82
regulation of commercial broadcasting, 49–51

Robinson, Walter "Robbie," 21
Roosevelt Institute, 67–77

S

sensationalism, 15, 46
Sheikh, Ahmed Al, 93–98
Silver, Laura, 30–34
Simmons, Katie, 30–34
Simon, Scott, 55–57
Snowden, Edward, 9, 24–29
social media, how it is changing journalism, 19–23
Stocking, Galen, 90–92
Stray, Jonathan, 35–42

T

target marketing, 108–110
tech industry, media coverage and promotion of, 58–61
Telecommunications Act, 43, 45–46
Theranos, 55–57
Tomasi di Lampedusa, Giuseppe, 23
Trump, Donald, 7, 9, 35–42, 79, 86, 87, 90–91, 93, 94–95, 96, 114

W

Walker, Mason, 90–92
Wilson, Steve, 14

Y

York, Jillian, 28

Z

Zeta-Jones, Catherine, 62, 63